NORWICH

The Golden Years

1900s to 1980s

CONTENTS

The publishers would like to thank the following companies for their support in the production of this book

Main sponsor

R G Carter

Bowhill & Elliott

Broads Tours

BBC Fire Protection

First published in Great Britain by True North Books Limited

England HX3 6SN

01422 244555

www.truenorthbooks.com

Copyright © True North Books Limited, 2015

All rights reserved. No part of this publication may be reproduced, stored in a retrieval system, or transmitted in any form, or by any means, electronic, mechanical, photocopy recording or otherwise without the prior permission in writing of the Copyright holders, nor be otherwise circulated in any form or binding or cover other than in which it is published and without a similar condition being imposed on the subsequent publisher.

INTRODUCTION

'Norwich – The Golden Years' is the latest publication in our 'Memories' series of publications, covering nostalgic reflections of towns and cities throughout the UK. Within the pages of this new book we will be meandering through a pictorial cross-section of life in Norwich over the last 100 years or so, to help us recall memories of a different era.

Many of these photographs are unique and will inevitably remind us of events, experiences and memorable moments in our lives. Norwich city centre has streets that still carry a lot of their medieval charm, including some remains of the ancient city walls and a wealth of historic buildings. The Norman Cathedral is one of the finest in England, with its magnificent cloisters and Cathedral Close. The majestic castle with its fine 12th century keep is prominently situated overlooking the city. All this contrasts with the modern including the state-of-the-art Forum, Riverside development, and the city's two shopping malls. This is all linked together with some of the most attractive streets in the country including many cobbled streets, alleys and lanes. Norwich also has some fine open spaces, including the wonderful Riverside Walk and Chapelfield Gardens.

Norwich businesses make the city one of the top shopping destinations in the UK and offer a mix of both high street names and individual boutiques, as well as the largest permanent open air market in England. The city has a wide selection of hotels and its main attractions lie in close proximity to one another and this helps to make Norwich what it is today - a beautiful, relaxed and vibrant city. It marries its rich history with contemporary lifestyles.

But this book is principally about nostalgia and what makes Norwich special. Whether you remember shopping in Curls famous department store or watching the construction of Norwich City's stands by local firm R.G. Carter, every facet of Norwich life finds a place in this book. Enjoy this unashamed journey down memory lane and wait for the memories to come flooding back.

TEXT ANDREW MITCHELL, TONY LAX AND STEPHEN FIRTH
PHOTOGRAPHS TONY LAX
DESIGNER CHRIS THORPE
BUSINESS DEVELOPMENT MANAGER PETER PREST

A SLICE OF PRE-WAR NORWICH

Situated at the end of Tombland, where it merges with Wensum Street and Palace Street, today the Maid's Head Hotel continues to present an attractive and imposing presence on the right hand side as we look towards it as it appeared a century ago. Parts of the hotel date from the 13th century and it is an amalgam of several buildings. It is said that Horatio Nelson of Trafalgar fame and the brave World War One nurse Edith Cavell have been guests. Even Queen Elizabeth I laid her head on a pillow here in 1587 and several ghosts are thought to wander the corridors. Over the road, there is still a pair of eccentric figures guarding the doorway, though the façade has had something of a makeover.

An open-top tram leads the way as traffic crosses Fye Bridge after the east side of the bridge had been rebuilt in the early 1900s. Fye Bridge is arguably the oldest river crossing in Norwich and is the gate to the North of the City known as "Norwich Over the Water". This bridge was also the site of a cucking stool for ducking lawbreakers and undesirables. On the right, off Fye Bridge Street, is the three-storey F.J. Bugg Ltd factory on the Quay Side and on the left we can just see the elegant tower the Church of St Clement the Martyr, which dominates the eastern end of Colegate.

These images from Oak Street in the mid 1930s, give a real nostalgic flavour to typical city street life in that pre war period. At 93-101 Oak St, on the west side just north of the Inner Link road was a rather run-down block of shops and tenements occupying what had been a mansion of considerable size. Built of brick late in the 17century, it was of two main storeys, with a basement and attics. Rusticated quoins, small keystones above the windows, and a stringcourse marking the division between the two floors relieved an otherwise austere facade. An opening wide enough to admit carriages divided the ground floor into two unequal parts and gave access to Bath House Yard at the rear. The house, although listed under Section 3 of the Housing Act, 1949, was cleared away some years after the Second World War.

Left: In between Nos 103 and 119 were located no fewer than seven yards. Some were named after neighbouring public houses, while others no doubt commemorated early residents or owners. One of the yards was named after the Key and Castle pub. The landlord at No 105, Oak Street was at one time William Sheward, who in January 1869, confessed to having murdered his wife some 18 years earlier while living in Tabernacle St (now the west end of Bishopgate). Sheward was subsequently hanged at the old City Gaol at St Giles' Gates on 20th April 1869 - the first execution to be held in private in Norwich.

Left: Almost opposite to Flower Pot Yard stood Nos 156-158, a centuries-old building of which one of the most notable features was the chimneystack. It was of brick, both shafts being octagonal and sharing a neat base. The windowless dormers were not so attractive, however, and gave rather a vacant appearance to the building. Perhaps the Window Tax had something to do with this. At the time of the Blitz, the raids did such extensive damage to this property that it was found necessary to clear the whole site shortly afterwards. In later years, the larger houses which lined the streets, many of them of Tudor origin, had become divided up into small tenements.

Right: A few yards to the south of the Royal Oak was Old Brew Yard. This, one of the widest yards then existing in the city, took its name from an early nearby brewery, as also did Little Brew Yard next door. The houses on the south, which divided one yard from the other, probably dated from the 17th century. The photograph from July 1937, shows the west side of the yard, formed by the houses facing Oak Street. No 126, on the right, was the oldest, having flint and brick rubble walls and an old English plain tiled roof. Beyond Little Brew Yard is Jenkins Lane, a narrow alley that leads past the site of 19th century Oak Terrace and eventually to the Gildencroft.

A landmark Norwich scene only a few days earlier, was replaced by a building site during the rebuilding that took place around Norwich market in July 1938. Workmen had already started work to transform the Norman site.

In the photograph top right, we can see the excavation process well underway in the old fish market area at the rear of the "Tin Hut". Not a hard hat in sight, as tons upon tons of rubble was removed from the market reconstruction area. Little did they know, at the time, but this would pale in significance compared to the devastation caused by German bombers only a few short years later. When this photograph was taken looking north towards St Peter Mancroft parish church, which stands on a slightly elevated position next to the market place.

During the upheaval, traders had to continue to work so temporary stalls were erected around the vicinity. In the image, bottom left, we can see local Norwich folk go about their daily business in an area known as the "Sand pit" around the time of the demolition of the old Municipal buildings.

Lyons' Swiss Rolls

VG 7916

This is a classic picture from the mid-1930s, above, showing the business premises of W.F.Smith & Sons in King Street. What could be a Morris Oxford Sixteen is parked outside the multi-functional business premises. Not only were Smith & Sons the official Morris Service Station and Radiator Specialists, but they were also tin, iron and zinc workers and general hardware men. As long ago as the 14th century on this site was Berney's Inn; John Berney of Witchingham being entered on the roll of burgesses at that time. In the 16th century this was the city house of Heydons of Baconsthorpe.

In the photograph to the left, we can see the same building, nos 86-90 King Street, almost 50 years later, after being refurbished.

Nos 91 and 93 stood on the north corner of Green Lane. The former was a house and the latter a shop, both occupying what was originally one dwelling probably dating from the 17th century. They had a picturesque appearance due to the unusual arrangement of gables. John Crome the artist would have been familiar with the building, for he and his family lived in one of a terrace of houses south of the Green Lane entrance. These houses were demolished at the turn of the century, to be replaced in 1901 by six cottages known as Layers Terrace. These in their turn were pulled down in 1962 under a slum clearance scheme, and the Inner Link road subsequently passed across the site. A rectangular stone plaque rescued from the front wall of No 89 (the end house of the terrace) is now in store at the Bridewell museum. The chap looking in the window is looking every inch the stereotypical, Chicago gangster, private eye or newspaper reporter seen in the films of the time.

Looking down Guildhall Hill from St Giles Street in 1919 illustrates what a remarkably busy and thriving city Norwich was in those days just after the First World War. However, it was not all good news as many people found things difficult in peacetime. There were families who had lost breadwinners and loved ones and were finding it hard to make ends meet. On the other hand, some folk were doing well enough, as can be seen from the evidence presented by the car outside the organ showroom. Only someone from the well-heeled middle classes could afford an open topped tourer like the one we see turning the corner.

This open topped tram did not have many more journeys to make on the loop line along St Catherine's Plain before the system closed. Not surprisingly, the upper deck was empty. Let's face it, who would want to ride up there on a February day in 1934 or any other year? If you wanted to brave the elements, 26 hardy folk could sit on the upper deck of the open trams. Work on constructing the tramways in Norwich began in June 1898 and the first electrified service came into being on 30 July 1900, run by Norwich Electric Tramways, a subsidiary of New General Traction. A generating station was built on Duke Street to supply power for the scheme.

You get an excellent panoramic view over the Wensum valley and into the city from a vantage point on St James' Hill. The valley first began to take its present shape at the end of the Anglian glacial period, some 425,000 years ago. Prominent in the south west is the spire of Norwich Cathedral. The highest part of this spur of Mousehold Heath is home to Norwich Prison that opened in 1887 on the site of the old Britannia Barracks, the former home of the Royal Norfolk

Regiment. In more recent times, Ron Saunders, Norwich City's manager (1969-73), used to send his players up and down the hills here as part of their training regime. It must have worked as he guided our boys into the top tier of English football for the first time in the club's history in 1972. This picture shows people returning from celebrations held as part of George V's Silver Jubilee in 1935.

Pitt Street can be found just to the north of the city centre. Today it is home to a few businesses and a handful of residential properties. The older ones in our photos have gone, thankfully so in the case of those in Blakeley's Yard as these were slum homes in the 1930s where the standard of living was low. Facilities were very dated and the conditions in which people had to exist were not to be recommended. Many of these two storey buildings had an attic room and a large number dated back to the early 19th century. A mix of road widening schemes and enemy action during the last war took their toll here, but the last house of this type was not demolished until 1973.

Above: The companion photograph shows St Mary's Alley where Smith & Carman sold Steward and Patterson's bottled beers, just down from 6-8 Pitt Street where a poster was displayed advertising a screening at the Empire Cinema on Oak Street. It starred Jack Holt (1888-1951), an actor who had a long career in low budget Hollywood movies in both silent films and talkies.

Right: The photographer would have been standing on the corner of Duke Street and St Marys Plain to take this nostalgic image from 1937. It is possibly mom and daughter that are cycling past what was to become Robin Hood Cycles on the corner of Pitt Street and Muspole Street. On the left is the entrance to the 'Snug' of the 'Whip & Nag' public house. Some of these timber framed buildings could date back to the 15th century and are still intact and standing today, although the pub and the shop have long gone. This portion of Pitt Street was later to be added to Duke Street.

Left: The sun was shining on St Stephen's Road in mid May 1939. Yet, the storm clouds were gathering elsewhere over Europe. Italy and Germany signed a 'Pact of Steel', a military and political alliance between the two Fascist states that was virtually a declaration of war in itself, though the real thing would not start until September. Low's garden supply shop, selling seed and fertiliser to help householders beautify their lawns, would not be of interest to people in creating pretty gardens for many years to come. Instead, the 'Dig for Victory' campaign would see plots of land being turned over as the nation gave up its daffodils and petunias and turned to cultivating potatoes, carrots and cabbages instead.

Below: It is so long ago now that we have to be well into our dotage to recall Bank Plain as it was in 1936. Those were the days of small, individual shops where the owners often lived above their workplaces. Some might just recall the names that traded from here. At the end of the row we had Spelman's, with Norton's tobacconist's alongside. James Bloomfield's antique store was holding a closing down sale at No 15, next to the bookshop at The Church House.

Taken on the same day in late February 1938, the northeast corner of the market is shown as viewed from two different angles. One shot (below) was taken from Guildhall Hill and we can clearly see that the outfitter Hope Brothers was holding a sale and that, further to the right, Lyons was advertising its tasty Swiss Rolls, whilst H Samuel sold its jewellery and watches beneath. Lloyds Bank occupied the light coloured building in the centre. The above image was taken across Gentleman's Walk during a road widening scheme. Facing us are the shop fronts belonging to Willerby's, Dean & Palmer and the funeral director, Chamberlin. The Guildhall is situated to the left. Once the hub of city government, it also housed the assizes and magistrates' court until 1986.

This clutch of pictures all date from 1934. Showing different views of St Peter's Street as parts of it looked over 80 years ago, it is difficult to equate these with the scene close to City Hall and markets that we now have. Garland's furnishing and upholstery workrooms stood next to the entry to the yard belonging to the former Pope's Head pub. The Beehive at 7 St Peter's Street was another old 'watering hole', housed in a late Georgian building. The cars parked below the banner advertising the hardware store's closing down sale have registration plates that include one marked with the prefix NG. That vehicle was registered in Norwich, but its neighbour to the right shows VC, meaning it was a visitor from Coventry.

Above: This photograph is a reminder of one of Norwich's most popular hotels, visited by the great and the good during the 80 years it was open. Prime Ministers including Harold Macmillan and Harold Wilson have stayed at the Royal Hotel since it opened in November 1897. The grade II listed building you see today was built to replace an old coaching inn of the same name which stood on Gentleman's Walk overlooking Norwich marketplace. The new site in the area now called Agricultural Hall Plain was at the heart of Norwich's commercial district. The 'Royal' was designed by the Norwich architect Edward Boardman, who was one of the most successful Norwich architect in the second half of the 19th century. In this image from May 1935, we can see the hotel adorned with decorations for the Silver Jubilee celebrations of that year. The young man to the right of the hotel entrance below the 'Cross Here' sign, had to keep his wits about him, as he was stationed there by the tramway company to set the points for outward bound trams heading either for Magdalen Road or Prince of Wales Road. During the 1970s the hotel's fortunes began to fall into steep decline and the hotel closed its doors in 1977 and was subsequently used as a business centre.

PLACES OF WORSHIP

St Benedict Street has four medieval churches within 250 metres of each other, and there are three more on adjacent Pottergate, so it is no surprise that some of them are surplus to requirements; in fact, all seven are now redundant. St Swithin is one of the smallest, but it was already derelict in the 19th century. The tall, elegant tower, with the porch built directly into its south side, was taken down as unsafe in 1881, to the benefit of the adjoining alley, which until then had been barely a yard wide at that point. In this photograph from 1937 you can see the south side of the church was once at the hub of a flourishing parish. After the war, as with many Norwich churches, St Swithin was left to rot, being used as a furniture warehouse, until it was born again in the 1980s as the Norwich Arts Centre.

To the rear of the Church down St Swithin's Alley, this 17th Century building has a thatched roof which unusual for the city. This photograph was taken in June 1938 and the building has today been restored to its former glory. The beautiful gabled houses glimpsed on the right are long gone. When you leave the church, it is worth wandering down the lane to the west of the church, where the tower used to be.

Right: There are no winners in a war: just losers and those who lose even more. Our enemies lost countless thousands in attacks over Cologne, Hamburg, Dresden, Berlin and other cities. Our losses were considerable during the era we came to know as 'the Blitz'. Only those who lived through that time can truly appreciate what it must have been like to be on tenterhooks night after night as firestorms raged and death whistled down from above. We lost many precious buildings, particularly during the 'Baedeker' attacks when assaults were made on historic rather than strategic targets, as Hitler strove to break British morale. In late April 1942 our Anglican Cathedral was hit, but such actions tended to stiffen our resolve rather than dent it. Here we can see a service being held in the building's remains as the congregation metaphorically stuck its tongue out at the enemy.

Standing proud in the heart of Norwich, is the Cathedral of St John The Baptist on Uthank Road, the second largest Catholic cathedral in the country. The architect Patrick Palgrave-Moore has described it as 'perhaps the finest example of Victorian Gothic revival in this country', and here in this photograph from 1955 we can see why. It was gifted to the city of Norwich by the fifteenth Duke of Norfolk. At the Duke's request it was designed in the Early English style of the thirteenth century. The cathedral was constructed between 1882 and 1910 to designs by George Gilbert Scott, Jr. as a parish church dedicated to John the Baptist, on the site of the Norwich City Gaol. The rectory adjoins the church, which occupies a commanding site immediately outside St Giles' Gate. This is a rare view of cars crossing the 5-way junction that has completely changed and is unrecognisable today.

Right: The Anglican Cathedral of the Most Holy Trinity is home to one of two bishoprics to be found in the city; the other being the Catholic one that is dedicated to St John the Baptist. The most complete Norman Cathedral in England and one of the finest examples of Romanesque architecture in Europe, Norwich Cathedral is one of England's finest Cathedrals. This photograph of the C of E building shows it off in all its majestic glory. Building it began way back in the late 11th century on the site of a Saxon settlement and two other churches. The work was completed in 1145 and, although there were some alterations made over the next few centuries, the Cathedral has stood since 1480 without any significant change to its fabric. It also has the second largest cloisters, only outsized by Salisbury Cathedral. The cathedral spire, measuring at 315 ft or 96 m, is the second tallest in England despite being partly rebuilt after being struck by lightening in 1169.

Below: St Benedict's Street has five medieval churches along it, and they all have characters of their own. We can get a good view of St Margaret's Church and its elegant 14th century tower from this 1938 photograph, however as the trees have grown over the last 75 years since this image was taken; it is impossible to get the same clear view today. Although damaged by raiders during the war, losing all its Victorian glass, it was later repaired, the tower in 1948, the remainder by 1951. By January 1977, the church had come under the threat of redundancy and eventual demolition by the Brooke Report. Fortunately this did not happen, however, the building was subsequently stripped of its furnishings and by 1981 it was in use as a gymnasium. After lying empty it is now an exhibition space, also used for antiques fairs.

Above: The noble structure of St Peter Mancroft dominates much of one side of Market Square, but this view of it is partially obstructed by The Forum these days. The church's history can be dated back to the middle of the 15th century, though it does have a Norman foundation going back almost another 400 years. St Peter's bells are the inspiration behind a legend that tells of a nobleman who fell on hard times and was about to rob his brother, but was persuaded not to commit such a dastardly act on hearing a beautiful peal ringing out. Whatever the truth of the story, a jug of ale was subsequently provided for bellringers every Christmas Eve. The statue in front of the church of Sir Thomas Browne, the 17th century philosopher and physician, was sculpted by Henry Pegram (1862-1937) and unveiled in 1905.

Right: Coslany is a small sub-district of the city where we can find St Mary's Church on the Plain that bears its name. It is probably the former parish church of this Anglo-Saxon settlement and its tower must be at least 1,000 years old. It lay derelict at the end of the 19th century, but was revitalised during Edwardian times. However, this resurgence did not last long and the church fell out of use by the time the Second World War began, which was only a couple of years after this picture was taken. In more modern times the building has been home to an internet book company, a publishing business and an artists' studio.

Right: St Mark's in Lakenham is one of our 'village' parish churches, as those outside the city walls are known. It was built in the 1840s at a time when a revival in Anglican worship was spreading from Oxford. Its impressive rood loft and screen, installed in 1910, attract many admirers to pay a visit. The paintings, completed by Temple Moore, were based on designs by George Bodley. The church was damaged by fire in 1944 during an air raid. Parishioners stood bravely inside the building, wielding brooms and beating out flames on the burning timber as they fell from the roof above. Their actions saved the day.

Left: We are looking across the River Yare, about three miles from the city centre, at a tranquil scene in which the parish church of Thorpe St Andrew Episcopi occupies centre stage. This is the sort of image that English landscape painters love to produce to adorn the tops of chocolate boxes, though they might wish to first airbrush out the pair of old charabancs parked up on the right. Although we cannot see it properly from this angle, the church boasts the remains of a medieval tower to go with the Victorian one we have in this picture taken from the south bank of the river. The handsome 150 foot high spire is no longer with us, becoming unsafe as a result of damage during the wartime blitz. It was removed in 1944.

CARTERS CRUISES

EVENTS AND OCCASIONS

Stalls and Merry-go-rounds at the annual Easter Tombland Fair, in Norwich, around the mid-1950s. It is thought the fair dates back to the Norman times and was established for trade, bringing in large crowds from across the country. In later years the fair remained, but simply as a pleasure related event. Those old enough to remember the Easter Fair may recall the wall of noise, vivid colours and the smell of the generators, sharply contrasting with the sweet aroma of candyfloss and toffee apples. There was something for everyone, whether you were knocking cans off a shelf, sliding down the Helter-Skelter or trying not to be sick on the Waltzer, there was a special excitment and anticipation that only came round once a year. For those who preferred aerial thrills, there was the Big Wheel or Paratrooper as can be seen in this photograph below from 1965.

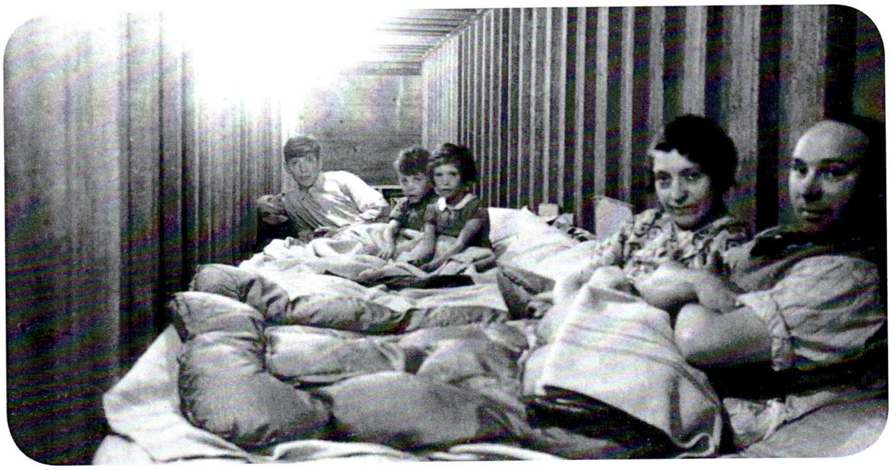

During the last war procedures for precautions during an air raid had been practised diligently. It was just as well for Charles Harmer and his family as they were able to take refuge in a purpose built shelter during the aerial attacks on our city. Mr Harmer was the caretaker at Churchman House, the city registry office and, though everyone pictured was safe, it is obvious from their expressions that the children were frightened and puzzled. Churchman House narrowly avoided destruction, but householders on Somerleyton Street were not so fortunate. Some houses were destroyed in April 1942 and the remainder hit again less than three months later. Norwich Hospital was also bombed that summer, with 120 beds being lost and operating theatres destroyed. Here nurses tried to salvage what they could.

The message is quite clear 'God Save The King & Queen'. This banner was part of the street decorations prepared in readiness for the Silver Jubilee celebrations in May 1935. The people of Norwich were about to start a week of festivities to mark 25 years on the throne by King George V and Queen Mary. The photograph is listed as Rampant Horse Street and much was at stake, as a prize of a silver cup was awarded for the best decorated Street. The ice cream seller is not too worried about the occasion as long as people buy from him. He has his own message 'Stop Me Buy One'.

Above: How much time and effort must the staff at Loose of Norwich spent creating these marvellous costumes for the carnival in July 1931? They are seen posing here for the cameraman as seven Wedgwood Portland vases. All participants were happy to take part as the money raised was for the Norwich Hospital fund. Crowds lined the streets, as the floats set off from Newmarket Road and passed the old Regent Cinema on Prince of Wales Road accompanied by music from the marching band of 4th Norfolk Territorial's. The day ended with "Thurstons" fun fair, set up at Grove Meadow.

Left: No bull this is a genuine photograph from 1937 of a stand-off in the Haymarket between this bull and his friend and pursuers. On their way from the old cattle market some cattle had stampeded from Orford Hill. These two ended within the protective chains of the garden, next to the statue of Thomas Browne, for an hour before they could be persuaded to enter the float that had been brought round for them. Perhaps the greatest change here in recent times took place in 1972 when the garden and lawn surrounding the statue were replaced by a paved concourse with seats and a "water feature".

The old tramway shelter and timekeeper's office was a great place to attach ribbons, flags and bunting on special occasions, as we can see in these two photographs taken only a couple of years apart. In 1935, Norwich celebrated 25 years on the throne by King George V and Queen Mary, with a week of festivities and great public rejoicing, and in May, 1937, the shelter was a central point in street decorations for the coronation of King George VI and Queen Elizabeth. The shelter was built in front of the Orford Arms Hotel on Orford Place, in 1928. This was essentially the hub of the tram service, which had seen trams running since July 1900. A comparison to today would place the shelter in the middle of Red Lion Street, outside the corner of Debenhams.

A sad day for theatre lovers as here in this photograph we see the remains of the Theatre Royal after a major fire on 22 June, 1934. Two days later and people are still strolling along Theatre Street trying to get a glimpse into the burnt out shell of the building. The clean up operation had started after the fire which spread so that within an hour the whole theatre was involved. Two open wagons from Pointer's, are parked outside the entrance as burnt debris is passed out of a first floor window. Proprietor, Jack Gladwin, was faced with the choice of abandoning it altogether or completely rebuilding. Fortunately for Norwich he chose the latter course, and on 30 September, 1935, the new Theatre Royal, after designs by architect W.H.Barton, opened with a production of The White Horse Inn.

Meaning 'Body of Christ', Corpus Christi is a special day in the calendar of particular significance for the Catholic Church. It is a celebration of the Eucharist, commemorating the Last Supper when Jesus ate with his disciples the night before he was crucified. Consequently, the feast day is celebrated on a Thursday. However, its timing is somewhat at odds with the Easter period as Corpus Christi is observed on a later date. In 1938, it occurred on 16 June, with processions and services held the following Sunday. Little girls in their white dresses and veiled headwear, holding posies of flowers, led the way from the Cathedral of St John the Baptist along Earlham Road to Heigham House. The scene was mirrored in Catholic communities up and down the land.

Don't look now but there is a stag flying through the air! Well not actually flying but being hoisted into position at its permanent home at No8 Orford Hill. For over a century a concrete stag surmounted on the 19th century building of Darlow's gun shop, but after a fire in January 1973 it had to be removed. On 19 June, 1984, a glass fibre replica was hoisted into place with the aid of a fire service. Immediately beforehand appropriate speeches were made by the Lord Mayor (Mr Stan Peterson) and the head mistress Mrs V Glauert of Blyth-Jex School where the new model had been constructed.

Above: Her Royal Highness Princess Elizabeth acknowledges the cheering crowds with a wave, as she makes her way past Orford House en route from City Hall to the Castle and then to Assembly House for lunch, with Lord Mayor, Mr Eric Hinde. This was the first visit to the city for the princess on 18 June, 1951, to open Norwich Festival of Britain celebrations and the Colman Gallery, Castle Museum. Crowds lined the streets and got the best vantage points they possibly could to get a glimpse of the future Queen as she passed. She concluded her tour of the city by visiting a silk mill and a shoe factory.

Below and right: There is no cause for alarm as fire crews spring into action outside the City Hall in these images from 1955, as this was just a display by the Fire Service for Civic Week. Two fire engines arrived and the escape ladder is run up - a dummy is lowered from the escape ladder by rope and the ambulance will arrive on cue to receive the "casualty". This adjacent picture shows someone attempting to move part of a lamp standard that the fire-engine had just demolished, having rounded the corner from Bethel St somewhat carelessly. This was not an intended part of the display. Some weeks later, the fireman responsible was apparently found guilty of driving his fire engine carelessly, had his licence endorsed and fined £3 by the city magistrates.

KEEP
LEFT

King George V and Queen Mary celebrated their Silver Jubilee on 6 May 1935. By then, the Royal House was known as 'Windsor' as the couple had abandoned the Germanic Saxe-Coburg-Gotha for obvious reasons during the Great War of 1914-18. It had been a popular move and one that helped secure public support for our monarchs during an era that saw the King's cousins assassinated in Russia and deposed in Germany when those countries got rid of their Tsar and Kaiser respectively. In one of this pair of pictures (left) we see spectators returning to the city via tram or on foot along Gurney Road, having just watched a review of the troops that took place on Mousehold Heath. In the partner photo, cadets from Watts' Naval School were leaving the parade ground and making their way along Chestnut Avenue. The school, originally called Norfolk County, was set up in 1874 near North Elmham to meet the educational needs of the sons of 'local farmers and artisans'. It closed in 1895 and was later bought by EH Watts. In the early 1900s it was turned into a Barnardo's home with special emphasis on training boys for a life at sea. It closed in 1953.

Above: Magdalen Street is recognised as one of the most important thoroughfare's in Norwich-over-the-water, and in this picture we can see the flags are out above Loose's Emporium store. Festivities are about to begin all over Norwich, as part of the Silver Jubilee celebrations in May,1935. Further along, Scott & Co Drapers have also made a bit of an effort. In a less festive showing we can see F. Lambert & Sons tobacconist shop next door to Loose's. Established in 1791, Loose's are a traditional family business that has been trading in Norwich for well over 200 years. In the part of the store that's nearest to the camera, they are advertising that they are specialists in China, Glass and Earthenware.

Right: Jarrold's department store, on the corner of Bedford Street and Exchange Street, was festooned in glory to celebrate the Silver Jubilee of George V and Mary in May 1935. The store won third prize in the commercial section for its display. This is one of the few independent stores to have resisted the takeover by bigger High Street names that has subjected similar establishments in other British cities to being swallowed up and losing their identities, becoming just more links in a chain. The company was founded in Woodbridge, Suffolk in 1770. How many of us have enjoyed the times when Father Christmas delighted kiddies with his visits here every December. Remember the special colouring books he gave us when you just added water to the pages to help 'paint in' the pictures? Magic.

Left: We all still remember 'Woolies', the original nickel and dime store where, for most of the last century, you could get cheap and cheerful goods that did not stretch the purse strings too far. Of course, in time future generations will regard Woolworth's as a period piece, just an item of commercial history from long ago. But, until then, let us recall the happy times searching for some bath salts or cheap aftershave to put in our parents' Christmas stockings. This store was on Rampant Horse Street and won first prize for business premises with its Coronation decorations in May 1937.

Right: Norwich was granted city status as far back as 1194. During the Middle Ages it grew in size and wealth, being once second only to London in its importance. The charter of 1404 allowed the city to appoint a mayor, two sheriffs and aldermen to run the business and affairs of Norwich.

The parade held on 6 June 1954 was held to mark this historical moment as the Lord Mayor made an official tour of the city. Sea Cadets marching along the streets were just one part of the formal turn out. Coincidentally, this was the organisation's centenary year as it had been founded in Whitstable in 1854. The local branch was formed in 1912 and has almost always been a notable feature on the River Wensum with a floating HQ.

Above: Celebrations were held in 1983 to mark the 150th anniversary of Norwich as a port. A flotilla of a variety of vessels sailed from Oulton Broad to the Hotel Nelson at Foundry Bridge, by way of Haddiscoe New Cut on 2 October. There were also races, as the one here between crews propelling assorted craft, some privately built and others sponsored by local businesses. The port, now considered by the Council to be defunct, was situated on the River Wensum and has a history going back to medieval times.

The Coronation of George VI on 12 May 1937 drew a sigh of relief from the establishment as it marked the end of the era that would become known to historians as 'the abdication crisis'. With a new king firmly on the throne, the problems caused by his brother, Edward VII, could now largely be put to bed. Celebrations across the country took place on the day that had long been earmarked to crown George's brother. The public cared little for that and was only too happy to celebrate the day in time-honoured style, with parties, dances, fine speeches and, of course, a parade.

The floats passing St Giles Church, on the corner of Cleveland Road, included Doris Pitt as an impressive Britannia, children on horseback and a vehicle announcing the qualities of the products of the Young's, Crawshay and Young's Crown Brewery.

The owners of the 14th century church were seeking £3,000 to aid the restoration of the building. That was a tidy sum, worth about three-quarters of a million in today's money.

R G Carter
Building for the future

Even as a little boy, Robert George Carter, the founder of the R G Carter Group, had few doubts about what he wanted to be when he grew up – he wanted to be a carpenter, like his grandfather. This was the very first of many wise decisions which have resulted in the R G Carter Group becoming the successful, well-respected company that it is today.

Robert George Carter spent his childhood with his widowed mother and her parents at Drayton. Young George, as he elected to be called (George was his grandfather's name) left school at fourteen and became a carpenter's apprentice, practising his new skills with the tools he had inherited from his grandfather. After completing his apprenticeship, he tried life in London but decided it was not for him. So he returned home and joined a long queue for work outside Youngs, one of Norwich's best-known building firms. One after another the men in front of him were turned away, but when George reached the front of the queue John Young's offered him a job on the spot. Clearly, even at that early age, he stood out from the crowd.

For the next few years he went from project to project and was involved in a number of grand schemes, such as rebuilding the stable block at Ditchingham Hall and constructing a new wing at Blofield Hall, where he worked with experienced craftsmen who displayed the high levels of skill and craftsmanship that were to become so important to George. In 1914, after the commencement of the Great War, George Carter joined up and served in France with the 126th Field Company of the Royal Engineers. He was lucky to survive the war. He was wounded twice, and it was feared that he had lost his sight during one gas attack; fortunately this proved not to be the case, but his health was permanently affected. His bravery earned him the Military Medal and the Croix de Guerre. Having refused a commission early in the war, he left the army as Sergeant, and within three days of being demobbed had found himself a job with the London building firm Scott and Middleton, working on the site of Caley's chocolate factory at Chapel Field, Norwich.

__Top:__ Craftsmen in the 1930s with R E Carter as a boy and apprentices learning traditional skills. __Right:__ R G Carter, (1892 - 1966) founder of the company.

George's ability quickly earned him promotion to foreman and then to general foreman. Like most builders he did a few private jobs in his spare time, and a lady named Mrs. Raikes asked him to fit new windows; by the time the windows were fitted George had fallen in love with Mrs. Raike's cook Florence Rolfe, a quiet, gentle woman, daughter of a farmworker from Diss. The young couple were married in 1921. That same year Scott and Middleton's work at Caley's was complete and they asked George to go to Newark where they were to build a bridge, but George wished to stay with his new bride in Norfolk, so as an ambitious young man he decided to leave and concentrate on building up his own business.

From the outset, the whole family was involved in the venture; his uncles helped him financially, Florence acted as secretary, book-keeper and wages clerk and her brother Ted drove the horse and trolley before the firm's first motor lorry was introduced. George worked night and day to get his business up and running. He began by building cottages at the Stanninghall Tuberculosis Colony, followed by private houses including a semi-detached property at Rail View, Drayton (now known as 38 & 40 Taverham Road), one of which became the home of George and Florence, their son Robert Edward, born on 2nd December 1922 and daughters Betty, Mary and Ruth. By 1926 his half-sister Muriel Hall was assisting as his secretary.

In 1922 R G Carter carried out his first job for Bullard's converting buildings at the Anchor Brewery into garages as the brewery changed from horse-drawn vehicles to motor lorries. Ernest Bullard was more than satisfied with his work, and this was the beginning of a relationship that lasted until Bullard's was taken over by Watney's in 1963, with George Carter being invited to build several new pubs as well as undertake renovations and maintenance on others. George also built up a close relationship with another important Norwich brewer, Morgan's Brewery Co. Ltd. Among the many pubs built, extended or maintained by the firm for both breweries were the "White Hart" and the "Bush Inn" at Costessey, the "Red Lion" at Drayton, and the "Bricklayers Arms" at Bull Close, Norwich. The most iconic pubs worked on during this period were The Artichoke at Magdalen Gates, the Gatehouse on the Dereham Road, The Galley Hill - now a Beauty and Hairdressing salon - which was part of the Mile Cross housing development and the Constitution on Constitution Hill.

During the 1920s and 1930s, work included a number of village halls and church buildings, such as Sunday school rooms for the churches in Belvoir Street and Dereham Road, churches for the Christian Scientists and for the Christian Spiritualists, and refurbishment of St. Alban's Church at Lakenham (in conjunction with H Bullen & Son of Cromer); public buildings: the Eye, Ear, Nose and Throat block at the Norfolk and Norwich Hospital, the David Rice Hospital in Drayton and the Maternity wing at the Norfolk and Norwich; and in the late 1930's Norwich Grammar School.

The firm was also gaining a reputation for industrial and commercial work in addition to its housing expertise that covered everything from estates for private developers and local authorities to individual architect-designed properties. The firm first worked for Norwich City Corporation in 1925, building houses at the back of Magdalen Street to replace the slums of the Norwich yards, and their first big contract was for housing on the Drayton Road.

George worked hard but he always found time for his children, and was a strict but loving father. Where work was concerned, his guiding rule was that a contract had to be completed on time even if it meant working from six in the morning until ten in the evening during the summer months. When a contract was finished he liked to put up hoardings emblazoned with the firm's proud boast, "On Time Again"! His bricklayers were expected to lay 800 – 1,000 bricks in an eight hour day, and carpenters had to hang a standard internal door in an hour. George inspected how doors had been hung using an old penny to make sure that the space around the door – the "penny liberty" was exact. His workforce learned that he would not tolerate timewasters but would reward hard work. At a time when employment rights were minimal and employers could act in an arbitrary manner, George preferred to keep the same men together and was quite happy to pay for travelling time in order to keep gangs together. His ability to create loyalty among his workforce is demonstrated by the firm's record of long service and the fact that so many members of the same families were eager to work for R G Carter. All this created a family feeling within the business.

Above: *The original R G Carter offices at Drayton in the 1920s.*

George Carter's firm survived the depression of the late 1920's and early 1930's which put many builders out of business, but it was not an easy time. Some men had to be asked to leave; however, George tried to shed as few workers as possible, and this was appreciated by the men. In 1932 the worst was over and George decided it was time to turn the firm into a limited company, and so R G Carter Limited began, with a sound reputation based upon quality workmanship, prompt completion and first-rate service. At the heart of the new company lay its expanding workforce, a band of men who were not only talented tradesmen but also completely committed to furthering the firm's reputation. In 1935 the building firm of Herbert Bullen and Sons Limited was acquired by R G Carter Limited. George Carter was by now employing 250 men.

Three years later his son Bob, who had been educated at Norwich School, a popular and sociable young man as well as an enthusiastic cricketer, golfer and fisherman, joined the firm as an apprentice carpenter. Unfortunately his early career was interrupted, as his father's had been, by the outbreak of war.

Early in the war the firm was involved in the construction of a new naval base at Immingham, as a result of which the business obtained a steady stream of contracts for various Government departments, notably the War Office, the Air Ministry and the Admiralty. One of the more unusual jobs was a contract at Withernsea on Humberside which involved building a fake city, complete with homes and factories, as a decoy to draw German bombers away from the important target of Hull.

Above: *Bonds under construction by John Young's in 1952 by H. Moore. John Young's established in 1861, built both Thorpe Station and the Royal Hotel during the latter years of the 19th century. John Young's became part of the R G Carter group in 1967.* ***Picture:*** *John Lewis Partnership.*

Bob Carter returned in 1946, and after completing his apprenticeship he took a correspondence course in quantity surveying. He then started work in the offices at Drayton, which had now moved from Low Road to larger purpose-built premises in the High Road where R G Carter Limited remains to this day. By 1950 Bob Carter was actively running the company as Managing Director.

One of the main priorities after the war was the construction of housing, and R G Carter Limited played a full part in this, building 4,000 houses between 1945 and 1960, principally for local authorities. One foreman, Wilfrid Bone, was awarded the British Empire Medal for his contribution to the public housing programme.

The company constructed further pubs during this period including The Dial on the Dereham Road (now Tesco Express), The Barn at the junction of the Dereham Road and Grapes Hill – now Cane Furniture Centre - and the Bignold Arms at Hellesdon, now a Fish & Chip Restaurant, a number of school and college buildings in and around the city; the new north wing added to Norwich City College and School of Art in

Above: *Bob Carter (1922 - 1974).* ***Left:*** *Princes Street, Norwich renovated in 1957 by R G Carter to retain its Tudor exterior.*

Ipswich Road between 1951 and 1953 was the largest building put up in the city since the end of the war. Norwich Training College, a teacher training institution in College Road, destroyed by bombs in 1942, took out a lease on the 19th century Keswick Hall and contracted the company to carry out alterations, following this up a year later with a further contract to build a new east wing. This was opened in April 1951 by the H M the Queen, with George Carter in attendance.

Many important city landmarks which had been destroyed or allowed to fall into decay during the war were restored by the company, and their construction of the Colman Galleries at Norwich Castle, which were opened by Princess Elizabeth in June 1951 (when R G Carter was presented to Her Royal Highness) marked the emergence of the city from the gloom of the immediate post-war years.

In the early 1950s under Bob Carter's leadership, the company developed a highly professional approach and business began to boom. By the mid-1950s, R G Carter had become the largest building firm in Norfolk. Subsidiaries included Bullen's, Fishers, Blackburns and Drayton Stone Pits; 850 men were employed at Drayton, and 2,000 throughout the Group. Prestigious clients included Norwich Union, for whom the firm first constructed a block of offices and shops in Surrey Street in 1952, followed two years later by new offices at 19 Upper King Street. Norwich Union then announced major plans to redevelop the "island site" bounded by Surrey Street, Westlegate and All Saints Green, the intention being to re-house 2,000 office staff in a new L-shaped block. Before work on that project began, Norwich Union showed its confidence in the company by appointing them as main contractors for an office block at the lower end of Surrey Street. The company completed this three months ahead of schedule in February 1957. In 1958 the multi-million pound contract for the 190,000 square feet, ten-storey office block at All Saints Green for Norwich Union became the firm's second contract in excess of a million pounds; the first had been won the previous year for a new factory in King's Lynn for Campbell's Soups, where the successful execution of the original contract led to more work on the site, leading to the company setting up a branch office in King's Lynn in 1960.

George Carter died suddenly at his home, Drayton House, in Drayton on 30th September 1966 at the age of 74. The funeral was held at Drayton parish church on 4th October and in spite of the rain hundreds of people lined the route from the village centre to the church to mourn the loss of a great man.

Bob Carter succeeded his father as chairman of the Firm and a group of companies that covered an area of 500 square miles and employed 2,500 men. Bob was described as a perfect gentleman. Although not enjoying the best of health, he had a supreme sense of duty and a determination to uphold standards. As Managing Director, he had demonstrated the foresight and vision which had driven the business forward for a decade, allowing it to execute contracts larger and more complex than any it had previously handled and eventually to expand not only into a wider geographical area but also into other activities related to construction.

Above: *The founder, Mr R G Carter is hoisted by a tower crane to the roof level of the Norwich Union island. East Tower 1959.*

Under Bob Carter's chairmanship, the Group grew rapidly. Between 1966 and the Group's Golden Jubilee anniversary in 1971, turnover doubled to £15.3 million and the workforce increased to 3,000. Since the Group was carrying out more and more multi-million pound contracts, Bob Carter realised that much more emphasis had to be placed upon financial monitoring. In particular, he recognised that surveying was becoming increasingly important as a key control for the business.

Right: *County Hall.*

One of Bob Carter's ambitions was to initiate a more formal scheme of training within the Group which would provide greater opportunities for more people. He believed that better training would increase efficiency which in itself would create growth, and would also stimulate individual effort by enhancing the prospects of promotion. He introduced a training scheme at Drayton to improve the standard of apprentices; bricklaying was the first trade to become part of the scheme and young bricklayers spent three months on site, training with a general foreman. In October 1969 the Group Training Centre was opened at the premises in Low Road, Drayton, where the Group had started life in 1921 and remained in existence until August 1976 when it was superseded by the new CITB training centre in Norwich. The R G Carter Academy was re-established in 2006, working from the same original premises, and continues to the present day.

In 1967 the company acquired the old-established Norwich firm of John Youngs Ltd (where George Carter was first offered work after World War One). This company possessed a distinctive identity and valuable reputation and was run in parallel with R G Carter. Other acquisitions followed as the Group expanded throughout East Anglia. Norwich landmarks completed during this period include: the construction of the Anglia Square development at Magdalen Street, County Hall which was opened by the Her Majesty the Queen in 1968 when Bob Carter had the honour of being presented to Her Majesty. The Hotels Nelson and Norwich built in 1969 and 1971 respectively for Property Partnerships PLC, an eleven storey hospital block built between 1971 and 1974, the first major repairs for more than 500 years to the roof over the North and South aisles of Norwich Cathedral

***Above:** An aerial view of central Norwich in 1988 showing six Carter Group projects being carried out simultaniously - Sainsbury's on Queens Road, a car park for John Lewis, Sentinel House, Norfolk Town and staff canteen for Norwich Union and listed cottages in All Saints Green, also for John Lewis.*

using English oak in 1973, renovation work at Dragon Hall, various multi-storey car parks and numerous office blocks. R G Carter Limited and its associates also won a design competition organised by Norwich City Council for the redevelopment of the former Bally shoe factory site in Princes Street. The imaginative scheme provided for 27 houses and flats with shops and offices. At the same time, a second similar joint venture was agreed for the development of Colegate by building 39 large houses through two joint venture companies, Colegate Investments Limited and Colegate Developments Limited.

Bob Carter's health problems became so acute that he was advised that his only chance of recovery lay in heart surgery. Sadly, he failed to recover from the operation. He died on 21st October 1974 aged 51 leaving a widow, Mary, and four children: sons Robert George named after his grandfather, John, and daughters Jane and Louise. At his funeral service at St. Margaret's in Drayton, the Bishop of Lynn, the Right Reverend Aubrey Aitken, a family friend, described him as "a man of Norwich and Norfolk". More than 2,500 people attended his memorial service in Norwich Cathedral a few days later.

***Above:** Apprentices learning traditional skills at the R G Carter Academy.*

Bob's premature death was devastating not only for his family but also for the R G Carter Group. His elder son, Robert, was now, at an early age, thrust into a very senior role as Vice-Chairman and joint Managing Director. Whilst the business was sound, its rapid expansion, combined with a number of loss-making contracts, had left it seriously short of cash. But the Group had tremendous assets in the experience and expertise of its management and also in the loyalty of long-standing clients.

Robert Carter married Charlotte Miller, the daughter of a notable Norfolk architect, on 2nd May 1982, and exactly a year later their first child was born, named Robert Edward, after his grandfather, followed by Sophie, James and Camilla. Robert took over as Group Chairman that same year as well as continuing to run R G Carter Limited at Drayton as General Manager, a role he had undertaken since 1980. In his view, the Group's greatest strengths were its building expertise, skilled workforce and expanding reputation. In the increasingly competitive business environment of the early 1980's recession, Robert Carter was determined to give the Group a commercial edge and make it show a profit in every sphere of activity. The Group's traditional strengths enabled it to come out of the recession in a strong position and, having used the time to take the firm back to its roots, further expansion was now possible. The first new office was opened in Peterborough in January 1983, and Peterborough's development was a typical example of how the Group expanded from the 1980s onwards, with steady, progressive, organic growth, rather than growth by acquisition, as the key.

When work began on Colman's new packed goods store at Carrow in 1976, R G Carter Limited celebrated an association with Colman's stretching back 25 years. In 1979, the company gained a three-year multi-million pound contract from another long-standing client, Anglia Television, for the conversion of the former Post Office building in Norwich into a studio and offices linked to the existing premises completed by the firm ten years previously. At the University of East Anglia, the Group built the Sainsbury Centre for the Visual Arts to house Sir Robert and Lady Sainsbury's art collection. Described as a building with "panache" in the Architectural Review, it was opened in April 1978 to widespread acclaim from the national press and television, and won prestigious awards including the Royal Institute of British Architects (RIBA) Eastern Region Award and the Special Finniston Award for Structural Design.

In the early 1980s the Group embarked on a series of major prison contracts; the huge contract for Wayland prison, near Watton, was the largest contract the Group had ever handled. In 1979 the firm built the River End 9,200 capacity spectator stand for Norwich City Football Club to designs by J. Owen Bond. Then on 25th October 1984, the main stand at Carrow Road was destroyed by fire and the company was invited to build a new stand. Two Design and Build schemes were submitted and a contract was signed on 6th November, 1985. The new stand, named the "City Stand" was opened by the Duchess of Kent on 14th February 1987. Five years later, in 1992, the firm completed a third stand for the football club, the Barclay Stand rebuilt as a two-tier structure in accordance with the updated stadium regulations that followed the Hillsborough disaster, and this was followed by two further corner in-fill stands linking together all the new structures erected by the company. Continuing the firm's long association with Norwich City Football Club, R G Carter constructed the 8,000 seat South Stand which opened in February 2004, demolishing the original 6,000 seat stand built by the R G Carter Group in 1935. This was re-named the Jarrolds Stand.

In the summer of 1985 the company began refurbishing the Royal Arcade, built by John Young's nearly a century earlier, this was completed in 1990. In 1987, the company won the contract to build the new terminal building at Norwich airport, opened on 25th July 1988 by the Queen Mother. Also in 1987 the firm built the Norwich Sport Village which involved a unique form of undulating freestanding concrete shell structures covering the sports areas. At the same location the firm built the multi-million pound Aquapark complex in 1990. The company was also responsible in 1991 for the major refurbishment of Norwich's Theatre Royal, a contract lasting 44 weeks which was funded largely by business and public donations.

Above: *Aerial view of Norwich City Football Club Stadium showing all four stands built by the company between 1979 and 2004, clockwise, from top right, The River End (1979), City Stand (1878), Barclay Stand (1992) and Garrolds (2004) which replaced the original stand built by the company in 1935.*

The Firm developed a national expertise in the retail sector during the 1980's that led to the construction of the Budgens store at Sprowston (now Tesco Blue Boar Lane) and a new 6,400 metre superstore in Queen's Road, Norwich for Sainsbury's (on the site of the old Norwich Victoria Railway Station). In addition, the company worked for Tesco on the major refurbishment of a store in the heart of Norwich, close to the Guildhall, and the construction of a 5,750 square metre store at Harford Bridges on the outskirts of Norwich in 1996.

Among other major clients for whom the firm has carried out work over many years are Norwich Union, the University of East Anglia, Rhone-Poulenc who had taken over May & Baker, and Bernard Matthews. Business parks were a feature of the late 1980s and one of the first in the area was the Norwich Business Park at Whiting Road for one of the firm's long-standing clients, Frenbury Properties. In 1993, the company was appointed to carry out the main infrastructure works required at the St. Andrew's Business Park at Thorpe, developed to take advantage of the proximity of the new A47 southern bypass. On this site, the firm completed contracts to build both the 6,500 square metre office Roseberry Court and the print centre for Eastern Counties Newspapers. In 1994 the company became directly involved as landowners in the development of Longwater Business Park adjacent to the western section of the A47 bypass and in 1997 constructed a 5,570 square metre store for Sainsbury's in just 26 weeks. Development at the Park has continued, most recently the Next Longwater Home store opened in 2015.

In 1995, the year after the fire at the Central Library, fire swept through the Assembly House, destroying the roof and Georgian plasterwork ceilings. John Youngs spent 18 months restoring the building which re-opened once again in February 1997.

The Norfolk and Norwich Millennium Forum, designed by Michael Hopkins and Partners is a major piece of contemporary architecture in Norwich. It was built over two years to replace the Central Library that dramatically burnt down in August 1994. The Forum was opened by Her Majesty the Queen in her Golden Jubilee year where Robert Carter had the honour to be presented to Her Majesty. For R G Carter and for the city of Norwich it was a landmark scheme and an enduring concept. The Forum won numerous prizes including the prestigious RIBA Award for Architecture in 2004, the best in urban design by the Civic Trust and described as a "striking addition to the Norwich city skyscape".

In 2001 Norwich Castle Museum, closed for 18 months was given a new look by R G Carter with an outside glass elevator and the creation of new display areas. The building of Norwich Cathedral's Refectory was entrusted to the firm, the most significant new construction on Norwich Cathedral since the Middle Ages. The two-storey structure designed by Michael Hopkins and Partners has arching oak beams and cleverly displays the mediaeval stone and flint work of the Cathedral itself and was praised by the Fine Art Commission for grafting the future on to the past, enhancing but not harming it. The Refectory building was hailed by the Royal Institute of British Architects (RIBA) as one of the best examples of architecture in the East of England.

Between 2004 and 2006 R G Carter handed over new halls of residence to the University of East Anglia with cost-effective mono-pitched roofs for Browne, Ketts, Victory & Paston Houses. In 2000 the Norfolk Record Office was built adjacent to County Hall to house Norfolk's growing archive. In 2003 the Whitefriars office development built in the heart of Norwich with its glass façade incorporating features of the 14th Century priory on which it stands. Adjacent to this in 2009 the St. James Place development was handed over to Jarrolds. In 2007 the Theatre Royal re-opened following the Company's extensive refurbishment that transformed the city centre building. In 2010 the City's War Memorial works were completed to turn it to face City Hall. This gave the Lutyens designed memorial, in restored gardens, greater prominence and a more fitting environment for the taking of salutes from passing parades.

R G Carter's Jarrold Bridge, completed in 2012, collected an unprecedented six awards. After months of planning and off-site construction, the bridge was installed by a team from R G Carter in just a few hours over two days. Jarrold Bridge follows a "J"-shaped path across the River Wensum and was designed to require little maintenance whilst remaining strikingly aesthetic. The footbridge and cycleway links the Barrack Street development with the heart of the city.

Above: *Jarrolds Bridge.* ***Below:*** *Memorial Gardens.*

The scope of work undertaken by the R G Carter Group today remains as wide and varied as ever, embracing small works, maintenance and facilities management as well as major construction projects. Since 1982, under the chairmanship of Robert Carter, the Group has enjoyed the most successful period in its history.

The family tradition continues with his eldest son Rob Carter joining the firm in 2005 following his Master's Degree in Engineering from Durham University. His younger son James joined the firm in September 2008 with a degree in Architectural History from Edinburgh. A crucial element in this success is the whole culture of the Group as a family business which embraces everyone from the most junior apprentice to the most senior director and provides a strong element of security and stability for employees. Also, Robert Carter's firm belief in the continuous recruitment and training of apprentices – something which has always been maintained no matter how difficult things have been – has enabled the Group to sustain its traditional policy of internal promotion, which not only plays a key role in keeping the skilled and experienced workforce together but also helps the personal and family ethos of the Carter Group to be maintained. Thus, the firm established almost 100 years ago by Robert George Carter, is still building for the future.

Above: *The Forum, built by R G Carter is one of the most successful Millennium projects in the country. It opened in November, 2001, and is an iconic landmark and meeting place in the historic centre of Norwich.*

NORWICH STREET SCENES

It had taken a long time but life was getting back to normal in Norwich after the war when this elevated view of Rampant Horse Street was taken in the early 1950s. The bombings had taken a huge toll on the commercial businesses in the city centre and without the co-operation between retailers at the time many well known names could have been lost. Floors in other stores were made available by competitors for the unfortunate 'bombed-out' retailers. Perhaps the most significant of these was 'Curls' where all that was left after the bombing was a massive hole in the ground and a constant reminder of what had been before. Marks & Spencer had arrived on the scene but it was the rebuilding of Curls that seemed to crown the Norwich retail recovery. We can see from this photograph at the junction of Rampant Horse Street and Brigg Street, that work had begun to rebuild the store that would be ready to open its doors again in the Spring of 1956. In the background, on the left, we can just see St Stephen's Church and on the right, the Haymarket Picture House was still going strong. The advertising hoarding suggests we should try 'Splendo' a spread with a rich meaty flavour from Oxo. No thanks....I will stick to my Oxo cubes.

In the street scene that shows the Guildhall on the left, men's suits are being advertised for 47'6 (£2 7s 6d) or £2.38 rounded up in today's figures. This was a reasonable price without being dirt cheap during the interwar years. There was one outfitter who referred to himself as the 'Fifty Shilling Tailor'. Henry Price (1877-1963) built up a chain of shops after the First World War, selling suits for £2.50. The other view of the Guildhall also includes the Market and City Hall. The Guildhall pre-dated City Hall as the seat of local government. Built in the early 15th century, it acted as our administrative centre until 1938 and is the largest surviving medieval civic building outside London.

Right and below: The Tuns is a pub with a long history and in these two photographs we can see the premises either side of a major rebuild in 1937. As a public house it dates back to 1845 when the licensee was listed as Samuel Hinchley. In the earliest of the images, we can see two elegant ladies stolling past the lounge bar entrance on All Saints Green in 1936. The Norwich double-decker is heading out of the city on route to Hethersett via Newmarket Road. The Tuns was damaged by enemy action during a raid in April 1942 and was subsequently rebuilt. In 1970, Tina Clarke became one of the youngest licensee's at the tender age of 20, when she took over the pub. It was refurbished by Watney's in 1971 and became the 'Pig & Whistle', the name it is known as today, despite 5 or 6 name changes in between.

Below: This lunchtime scene is a reminder of the changes taking place on St Stephens Street in September, 1955. Opposite the end of Surrey Street we can see the new buildings which had been taken over by High Street chains Saxone Shoes and H. Samuel jewellers. Some ladies will remember the hairdressing salon of Andre Bernard. On the right is the new premises of well known Dispensing Chemists, Row and Taylor. A common sight in Norwich is the bicycle park. For many people in 1950s, the bicycle was the mode of transport for both work and leisure. Compared with today, few families could afford a car.

Below: Most people visiting Norwich come to Tombland and expect to see rows of graves or a cemetery or two in the vicinity. Sorry to disappoint, but the word has nothing to do with death, bodies or resting places. 'Tombland' is simply derived from the Old English for an open space. In Anglo-Saxon times the area was used as a market and administration centre before the Normans arrived on the scene. Today it is a lively spot with decent restaurants and bars. On 25 August 1954, the learner driver was negotiating Tombland corner from Queen Street, close to W Plowright's antiques' shop. This business was hit during an air raid in May 1943 and many valuable pieces were lost, but the proprietor rebuilt both his premises and his trade, though the estate agent's next door lay derelict for many years.

Post war life in Norwich was just getting back to normal despite evidence of the destruction caused in parts of the city during the conflict. These two elevated images give a snapshot view of Norwich folk going about their daily business in the area around Orford Place, Red Lion Street, Castle Meadow and Timberhill. In the years following the War rationing was still in place. Clothes rationing ended on 15 March 1949, however, times were still austere and it took until 1954 before rationing formally ended. With this people in the 1950s had more freedom over what clothes they wore. Business began to pick up significantly for the High Street fashion outlets such as Hepworths (converted to Next) and the Fifty Shilling Tailor (renamed John Collier) because most men still preferred the conventional suit in the fifties. They usually went to a tailor to be measured up. If they preferred to go for a pint there was plenty of choice, with the Bell Hotel, Orford Arms, or the Cricketer's all within a few yards of each other.

Below: The central part of the city was quite badly damaged during the last war and we lost many buildings, including Curl's store that stood on an island site in Orford Place. Seen from Rampant Horse Street, the City Engineers' department was busy attending to alterations to the sewage system in October 1953. This section of Norwich lay empty for over a decade, like some Quatermass pit. Rebuilding the department store was not completed until 1956, and it was then taken over by Debenham's in 1960. In the background the stand out building, is that of the Bell Hotel on Orford Hill. 'The Bell' is said to date from 1485, and was later one of the city's leading coaching inns. During the Second World War, the top floor was turned into dormitories for the American Women's Army Air Corps.

Below: The electrified tram system in the city lasted for only about 30 years. Introduced at the start of the last century, it had disappeared completely by 1935. The City Road service had been withdrawn in October, two years earlier, and here we can see the last pieces of track being removed from the carriageway in February 1934. The view is towards Bracondale, The Rose Inn on the left, a pub then tied to the Bullard brewery, is still standing on the corner with Queens Road. First listed as an ale house in 1856, it was taken over by Courage in 1972 and then Adnam's five years later. Bought by Dawn Hopkins in 2003, it became a free house and has since been refurbished. In the distance, to the right, you can see the west tower of St Bartholomew's Church on Ber Street. It is a remnant of the 14th century place of worship, desecrated in 1549.

Above: It was as far back as the Great War when widening St Stephen's Street was first mentioned. The idea came from the Great Eastern Railway Company that wanted to create a grander entrance to its Victoria Station, where Sainsbury's now stands. Things were put on hold until the 1930s, but nothing was decided until the Luftwaffe made the Council's mind up by destroying some of the buildings it wanted to preserve. Eventually, work was begun in 1953, though it took a decade to complete. This scene dates from March 1962 and also shows the old factory chimney belonging to Caley's Chocolates.

Left: It was at the narrowest part of Theatre St, opposite No 4, that a 1,000lb delayed action bomb fell during the early hours of 19 September, 1940, embedding itself deep into the subsoil. Fortunately it failed to explode and after much digging and delicate handling it was eventually defused and removed. The houses thus escaped damage at this time, but they were to remain only for another 24 years, for at the end of 1964 they were pulled down, No 4 being replaced by modern offices, the rest of the site being used as a "temporary" car park but earmarked for an extension of the civic centre. Here in this photograph from 1962 we can get a reminder of the former street layout.

Left: It is hard to get your bearings from this photograph taken in 1952, looking along Brigg Street, with Orford Place off to the left. The only recognisable building is the white one in the background, which was to become part of Marks & Spencer on Rampant Horse Street. Opposite that, at the time, was the building site of the new Curls store destroyed during air raids in 1942. When the remaining buildings were demolished Brigg Street was widened to traffic and Orford Place was reduced in width to be used by pedestrians only. We can see from the clock on the Gold Shop building that it is late morning yet there are very few people around, which might suggest it was a Sunday.

Right: These two photographs show retail premises at the junction of St Stephen's Street, Red Lion Street, Westlegate and Rampant Horse Street from over 50 years ago. In the older of the two images we can see the bike park opposite Marks & Spencer on St Stephen's Street in September 1955. This part of the street was destroyed by enemy action in 1942 and when the premises were rebuilt the front line of the buildings was setback several feet, to improve the entrances. In shot we can see the extension to the M&S store is part of the rebuild. In the second view from Red Lion Street, across the traffic light junction, we can see the retail premises opposite M&S, which is a mixture of old and new buildings at that time. In the Norwich Union building we can see the Dorothy Perkins shop and further up the street is the National & Provincial Bank (now Natwest Bank) and in front of that is a Cooks Travel Service unit. Today, there is no left turn in Westlegate as it is a one-way street.

PILCH
BUILDERS
LACEY

It took a long time to get things back on an even keel after the war. The economic cost of the hostilities was tremendous and left us in hock to the Americans right through the rest of the 20th century. Rebuilding homes destroyed by enemy action was a priority, but commercial considerations had also to be given. However, we were well into the 1950s before the 'new Norwich' looked like being created. In the Orford Place entrance from Haymarket, the company founded by Charles Gill on Trinity Street in the 1860s was hard at work erecting the skeletons of shops that would replace those lost to the Luftwaffe. In the view from St Stephen's Plain, also seen in 1954, some of the girders for the new Curl's store were in place. By the summer of the following year, much of the east side was completed, with Pilch's sports emporium, Benton's pharmacy and the Church of England Young Men's Sports Club all fully functional.

The construction of the new Curls store was well under way when this photograph (right) was taken around 1954/55. At last the giant hole in the ground, created by the German Baedeker Blitz in 1942, was being filled bricks and mortar to rebuild one of the city's premier stores. Since the bombing the site had been used as both a water tank and as a car park. Work started on rebuilding in 1953, however it was not completed until 1956. The No 86 double-decker bus and the car behind are manouvering around the roadworks into Red Lion Street, towards Castle Meadow.

In the second photograph (below) we can see the new Curls store just after the opening in the spring of 1956. The new store opened with entrances on Brigg Street, Orford Place, Red Lion Street and Rampant Horse Street and had 97,000 square foot of retail space. This was perhaps the most significant sign that Norwich had completed a full retail recovery after the dramatic events in 1942. The policeman on traffic duty in his familiar striped box was ready to control the traffic at the junction outside Curls. In the 1960s, Debenhams purchased the store but continued to operate it under the Curl Brother name until the 1970s, when they rationalised the brand.

store for Curls
T. GILL & SON
GILL
CONTRACTORS.
86
COSSOR
SELF MOTORING

The vast majority of people, even locals, could not direct you to Barwell Court. However, if you stepped out of the back door of Marks and Spencer, this is where you would be. It is just off St Stephen's Street and takes its name from that of a wine merchant who traded here in the 19th century. In 1955, the country was starting to pull away from the period after the war known as 'austerity Britain'. Rationing had finally come to an end in the previous year and the economy was really picking up. Shoppers started to spend money on what we now call 'white goods' as fridges and washing machines were becoming standard items rather than luxuries. We were on the brink of a new era and even M & S considered selling the new figure hugging blue jeans that were all the rage for young moderns.

A miserable damp day for shoppers on Brigg Street as they go about their daily business in this photograph from the early 1960s. The Ford Thames 400E van is parked outside the Universal Store at the entrance to the Haymarket. Brigg Lane (later Street) was named after staunch Royalist Augustus Brigg, in the 17th century. The lady with the headscarf crossing the street is more likely to be going to Dewhurst the butcher's rather than Halford's cycle shop. On the opposite side of the street on the corner with Orford Place is Lennards footwear shop ,who had branches in the vast majority of UK city centres. The street links Haymarket with Rampant Horse Street and is today pedestrianised and in the centre of shot would be two large staked trees with circular seats round the base.

TOBACCO
ADCOCK & SON LTD.
ADAMS
OPTICIAN
NEXT DOOR

Below: Things were changing in Norwich streets as town planners began to remodel many of the streets so shoppers would have a much more pleasant experience. Cars were banned from a number of the main shopping areas and many people came into the city centre on bicycles, as we can se in this photograph from October 1965. The first street to be pedestrianised was London Street. The Royal Mail van was allowed to pull up outside the impressive National Provincial building because they are on official bank business. Opie Street off to the left, is named after Amelia Opie a respected fiction writer of the 1800s who was born in a house on Colegate. In 1798 she married the painter John Opie and moved into a house which still stands on the corner of Castle Meadow. She died in 1853 and is buried in the Gildencroft Quaker Cemetery, off Chatham Street, by the side of her father.

Left: It is now over 200 years since Davey Place was laid out as a pedestrian thoroughfare. Seen here in the summer of 1961, when Elvis was telling us to 'Surrender' and Del Shannon to 'Runaway' at the top of the charts, people had been strolling along this route since 1813. It was created thanks to the ideas of Alderman Jonathan Davey, a prominent businessman and local politician. Linking The Walk with Castle Meadow, it was the first of our city's pedestrian only streets. In the foreground on the left, the three ladies are just passing the Electricity Service Centre shop. In the 1950s and 60s, they advertised themselves as the place to go for 'advice on cooking that's clean, efficient and very economical'. However, it doesn't seem that interesting to our three passers-by.

BUILDINGS, MONUMENTS & STATUES

You can almost hear Loyd Grossman's distinctive tones asking, 'Who could possibly live in a house like this?' The answer today is 'No-one', as Strangers' Hall is part of the Museum Service. It is one of the oldest buildings in the city and the fascinating Tudor house has been home to wealthy merchants and some of our Mayors over the years. The great hall has an impressive ceiling and mullioned windows. Its large communal space was formerly used for dining, sleeping and entertaining. The maze of rooms, furnished from different periods of history, is linked to the arrival in medieval times of Dutch Flemish and Walloon refugees, locally known as Strangers. They were encouraged to settle in the area in an attempt to revive the local textile trade.

Right: This rare image from 1934 shows the ornamental pagoda or pavilion that once stood near the centre of Chapel Field Gardens. Originally it was constructed by Barnard, Bishop and Barnard, the Norwich iron founders, from designs by Thomas Jeckyll as a showpiece for various exhibitions, being first erected at the Philadelphia Centennial Exhibition in 1876. In 1880 it was purchased by the city for £500, which was raised by public subscription. The garden's most conspicuous feature continued to attract the publics gaze, until it unfortunately sustained damage during the Second World War and was demolished in November, 1949.

People have been enjoying concerts at Eaton Park since the magnificent rotunda bandstand and pavilion was opened in 1928. Here in this photograph we can see a full house watching such an event in May 1932. Eaton Park has special historic interest and lies on South Park Avenue. The concerts are designed to allow people to enjoy the city's beautiful parks and free live music for people to while away their Sunday afternoons. It has recently had extensive renovation with the central Bandstand and surrounding circular pavilion and seating now looking as they must have been back at the time of this photograph.

These are very much 'before and during' images, showing the former Municipal Offices on the west side of Market Place in mid September 1934 and again during demolition. You might be forgiven for thinking that the later scene was one taken in the aftermath of a wartime bombing raid, but we did this ourselves in May 1938, when it was decided that new buildings were required. King George VI presided at the official opening in that same year. The new seat of local government had an orange hue, leading it to be nicknamed by locals as the 'marmalade hall'. The old buildings included the former Oxford Hotel in its right hand block, acquired in 1876. Eventually, the whole set of offices and chambers were purchased for use by the departments of the Town Clerk, City Engineers and Estate Surveyors.

Below: Around Norwich's Anglican Cathedral is Cathedral Close. Two tremendous gateways lead into the Close from Tombland. At one end is Erpingham Gate and the gate in this photograph is St Ethelbert Gate. This entrance is on Queen Street and the picture is taken outside Cambridge House in the 1960s. The Ethelbert Gate today is a reminder of the ruined church of St Ethelbert that preceded it before the violent riots of 1272, during the reign of King Henry III. The King required the city to replace the burned church of St Ethelbert with a new gate to the cathedral close, incorporating a chapel on its upper floor which was completed in 1325. The chapel above the gateway incorporates the music room of King Edwards School.

Above: This futuristic looking three-story building on All Saints Green is Bonds, one of Norwich's most prominent department stores, but today people will recognise it as the John Lewis store. Older readers may remember it as Bonds, taking its name from the founder who started the firm when he bought a small draper's shop in Ber Street. Bonds was started in February 1879

by Robert Bond when he took over Woodlands drapery shop at the end of Ber Street. The store was rebuilt with frontages on Ber Street and All Saints Green, with an arcade running in between in 1914. In the 1930s the store expanded by buying the Thatched Cinema on All Saints Green and using it as a restaurant and offices. However the buildings were damaged during the war with the Thatched Cinema being burned down. The store continued by using empty properties in Norwich and even sold stock from a fleet of buses on the car park.. After the war, in 1946, a new store was designed and building was completed in 1951. This is the store still favoured by local shoppers today, renamed John Lewis in 2001.

XRT 507

Left: This is a fabulous mid morning view from the early 1960s, of two of Norwich's most iconic buildings, looking across the northern edge of Market Place. A Ford Prefect 100c move across the picture on Gentleman's Walk, passing the imposing clock tower of the City Hall and the striking façade of the Guildhall. The Guildhall was constructed between 1407 and 1413 and served as the seat of city government from the early 15th century until 1938, when it was replaced by the newly built City Hall. Today, the Guildhall is the largest surviving medieval civic building in the country outside of London. The Grade II* listed City Hall was built to the highest standards, using superior materials and methods of its day. The clock tower was built in 1938 and stands 206 feet high from ground level. This is a nostalgic view from over 50 years ago but aside from the cars this view up Gaol Hill would be very similar today.

Right: Magdalen Street is one of the ancient roads in Norwich, it runs north from the cathedral and was, for many years, one of the main shopping streets in the city and it still contains a wealth of old buildings. Today however this end of Magdalen Street near the Colegate turning, is more to do with restaurants, fast food and charity shops. Back in the late 1930s, we can see from this nostalgic image, these buildings were occupied by some of the most well known High Street retailers. Seventy years on and both would be lost to the High Street. Building Nos 5 to 7 Magdalen Street dates back to the early 17th century and later became the Bull Inn. Described in 1743 as an ancient and commodious inn well situated for business with good rooms and stables fit for any accommodation at a reasonable rent. In this photograph, almost 200 years later however, rooms were one thing you couldn't get.

The old red bricked Grade II listed building, we today associate with Anglia Television studios was built as an Agricultural Hall in 1882 by Messrs J. W Lacey of Norwich. The architect was J. B Pearce and the opening ceremony was carried out by the Prince of Wales, later Edward VII. In his honour, the road leading down to Thorp Road from Agricultural Hall Plain, was named Prince of Wales Road. For much of the time the building served the City as an agricultural and exhibition hall until the Second World War. On 27 October, 1959 Anglia Television began broadcasting from the building, which externally appears much as it did on completion in November, 1882. Interestingly, when digging test holes in the basement for the foundations of the new studio building in 1958, the remains of at least three human skeletons were disturbed some 7-8 ft below the level of Crown Road. It was believed those burials surrounded a late Saxon church nearby.

Below: In this photograph we can see the main driveway and entrance into the elegant Norfolk and Norwich Hospital ('N&N'), founded in 1771 as a charitable institution for the care of "the poor and the sick". Established by William Fellowes and Benjamin Gooch, the hospital became a training centre for nurses in 1875, and was expanded in 1883 when a new main hospital building opened on St Stephen's Road. During the Second World War the hospital bombed on a number of occasions, including in April 1942, during the German Baedeker raids and 80 nurses and maids became homeless. In 1948 the National Health Service was founded and the 'N&N' became an NHS hospital. In this picture from 1955, we can see the building prior to the major expansion which took place in the late 1960s with the construction of a ten-storey maternity block, opened by the Queen Elizabeth. The grand old Hospital finally closed in 2003 after services were moved to the Norfolk and Norwich University Hospital and the building is now used as apartments.

Here we get a fantastic view from Thorpe Road of Norwich's fine railway station, which has changed little since this photograph was taken 60 years ago. The present building opened in 1886, built to a design by John Wilson. It is constructed of red brick and stucco, in a classic style, with an ironwork and glass concourse. The spacious porte-cochère would originally have sheltered passengers arriving and leaving by horse and carriage. It is topped by an imposing dome, covered in zinc tiles, seventy six feet high at its tallest point. The original station was opened by the Yarmouth & Norwich Railway (Y&NR) which was the earliest railway in Norfolk. The station has managed to retain its essential Victorian character, and is the only remaining one of the three which once served the city. Standing close to the River Wensum, across the Foundry Bridge from the city, it is a Grade II listed building, and acts as a terminus for trains from London Liverpool Street, as well as Great Yarmouth, Lowestoft, Sheringham, Ely and the city of Liverpool.

BRITISH RAILWAYS
NORWICH THORPE

Below left: The only things that give this away as an old photograph are the lack of road markings and the old styled black/white striped traffic lights, next to the towering South African War Memorial. The picture was taken just before the start of the Second World War and acts as a poignant reminder of the perils of conflict. The memorial to men of Norwich and Norfolk, who died in the Boer War, sits on an island at the junction of Castle Meadow and Market Avenue. Designed in 1903 by George Wade, it includes a bronze angel of peace with outspread wings on top of a granite and Portland stone plinth. This view has changed little in the last 85 years since the building of the magnificent Gurney's Bank building, named after the founding family. The classical style Grade II listed building, on the corner of Castle Meadow and Redwell Street, was the home of Barclays Bank until the late 1990s.

Above right: Many of those buried in unmarked graves at Earlham Road cemetary were soldiers from the Britannia Barracks. At that time mortality rates in the army were considerably higher than those of civilians of similar age, and in 1875 the Burials Board adopted a suggestion from a Mr. J.J. Winter that a piece of ground should be kept expressly for the burial of soldiers. He then proposed that a monument should be raised to the memory of soldiers who died while stationed in Norwich, which would record their names. Subsequently in response to the proposal, money was raised by public subscription and a statue, 'The Spirit of the Army', was unveiled by Lord Waveney in 1878. The statue was designed by John Bell, a sculptor from Suffolk, and made by Doulton's. By the mid 1920s the Cemetery extended as far west as Farrow Road. Earlham Cemetery opened on 6 March, 1856, with an additional 18 acres beyond Farrow Road laid out from the late 1920s onwards. By the time of this photograph in 1932 the cemetery reached its present size of 85 acres.

Below: Designed by Philip C Hardwick, this handsome edifice was built in 1866 at the top of what had just become known as Prince of Wales Road. Back then the classical style of architecture belonged to the Crown Bank. Hardwick had been commissioned by the bankers Harvey and Hudson who were impressed with his work on other banks and, in particular, when designing the great hall at Euston Station. The bank spectacularly failed a few years after opening here in Agricultural Hall Plain and, in 1875, became the General Post Office. It was extended in the early 1900s, taking on the appearance we have here in 1938. By the end of the 1960s, increased traffic in the vicinity and its awkward location saw the business move to other premises on Bank Plain. The building was sold to a property company in 1971. For the final quarter of the last century it was home to Anglia TV, but was later converted into apartments.

Above: This bizarre looking place on Westwick Street also delighted in the equally odd name of 'Monkey House'. The gable end is inscribed 'Removed from Whitlingham and rebuilt AD 1900'. Photographed in 1934, this building and its yard were used as the Corporation depot. It had been erected on the site of the medieval city wall at a spot adjacent to Heigham Gate. The Monkey House burned to the ground during the air raids of April 1942.

A before and after view of the Duke of Wellington statue, which was originally erected in the Market Place, in 1854. The Duke died in September, 1852. It was decided at a meeting to erect a statue in his memory, financed by public subscription. On completion, it was unveiled by the Mayor (Sir Samuel Bignold) in 1854, at a ceremony attended by 20,000 spectators. The bronze statue of the Duke of Wellington was sculptured by the artist George Adams. It originally stood in Gentleman's Walk facing the Castle, and was moved to its present position, on The Close in the grounds of Norwich Cathedral, in the January 1937. Judging by the cars in the background of the main image below, it is likely this photograph was taken shortly after the statue was relocated.

The message on the front of this building above is very clear, “A modern super cinema will shortly be erected on this site”. The reference is to the building of the Regal Cinema, by Thomas Gill & Son, in late 1937. Next door to the building on Dereham Road are a funeral service and St Benedict’s Garage.

In the main photograph right, we can see the ‘Regal’ on the day after the official opening in April, 1938, after a build of four and half months. It was operated by independent exhibitor Victor E. Harrison. Seating was provided in stalls and circle levels and there was a cafe for the convenience of patrons. The film showing was ‘Captains Courageous’ starring child star Freddie Bartholomew and Spencer Tracy. The cinema made the headline news in 1957 when it screened ‘Rock Around the Clock’ featuring the latest dance craze Rock ‘n’ Roll, starring Bill Haley and the Comets. Exuberant fans rioted and danced in the aisles and were chased out into the streets. The Regal closed not long after in 1958 and stood vacant before becoming the Mayfair Bingo Club which ran until 1990. More recently, it re-opened as Wetherspoon’s the City Gate pub. By August, 2014, it was operating as a bar & restaurant known as ‘Merge’.

The cameras were held on the castle battlements overlooking the city a quarter of a century apart to capture these panoramas. Looking west in April 1938, the City Hall tower was still in the process of being finished off. On completion, the official opening ceremony was conducted by King George VI and Queen Elizabeth on 29 October of that year. The Catholic Cathedral of St John's appears in the distance, while to the left is the distinctive sight of the church of St Peter Mancroft. Pictured in July 1963, we can now see the jolly awnings of the market stalls in the centre of the scene. To the left of City Hall, the new Central Library that opened the previous year is in view, but it would disappear in 1994 when gutted by fire. The latest library is now part of the Forum, built on the same site in 2001.

Red Lion Street, which links St Stephen's with Castle Meadow, passes Orford Place to Orford Hill. Here at No 16, now occupied by a branch of Marks and Spencer, stood the Livingstone Hotel. Starting life about 1720 as a Georgian mansion and once occupied by the Crosse family of medical practitioners, it became during the 19th century a temperance and commercial hotel, although after about 1921 it was largely used as stockrooms. We can see evidence of this in this photograph from August 1936. This and adjoining property, cleared away in 1961 for Littlewood's new store, occupied an historical site. George Green's tailor's and outfitter's shop, for instance, built facing the Haymarket in 1893, replaced the Star, known to have been a coaching inn as far back as 1684.

The photographer must have been directly in front of the Parish Church of St Giles on the Hill, when he took this picture in 1956. The three cyclists and the lone car are on St Giles Street at the junction with Bethel Street, in the centre of Norwich. Before 1900, number 68 St Giles' St (Churchman House) was listed as number 59 Upper St Giles' Street. Quite recently it was re-numbered again as 71 Bethel Street. The original Churchman House was built in the early part of the 18th century by Alderman Thomas Churchman, a prosperous worsted weaver. In 1875 it became the home of the Norwich High School for Girls for two years until the school moved to the Assembly House. After this the property was purchased by Sir Peter (then Doctor) Eade, an honorary consultant physician to the Norfolk and Norwich Hospital and later an Alderman of the city. After his death, the house then remained empty until purchased in 1919 by Norwich Corporation, who opened it two years later as the headquarters of the city's health department. In the late 1980s it underwent extensive restoration and conversion, and now this magnificent Grade II listed building is the main Norfolk Register Office.

At the foot of St John Maddermarket's churchyard still stands a relic of former times - the parish pump. The inscription giving the maker's name is now badly corroded, but it appears to have been a fountain pump patented by one John Shalders, whose business was situated in nearby Redwell Street. Similar pumps once lined the roads between Cringleford and Wymondham. These were placed there at the beginning of the 19th century by the Turnpike Trustees; their specific purpose was to provide water for experiments in roadmaking as well as for laying the dust. The significance of the situation of this one at the Maddermarket, with the land sloping towards it from the adjoining burial ground, was not lost on a former city analyst; he described it as "pure essence of churchyard". This charming photograph from July 1955 shows a smartly dressed young boy gazing upwards at the 7ft high pump, as it towers over him and an old Ford Pop passes in the background.

The entrance to the Royal Arcade and external façade, have changed little since the oldest of these two photographs was taken 80 years ago. Infact, it has been like this since 1846, when Joseph Stannard rebuilt the Gentlemans Walk entrance, creating the current three-arch entrance still used today. Inside, the 247 foot long covered avenue was designed and built by Dereham-born architect George Skipper in 1899 and initially it contained 24 shops, a pub and a Conservative club and still retains many of its original features, despite several renovations through the years. Over time, the stores names may have changed and Gentleman's Walk may now be pedestrianised, but once inside the grandour of the Art Nouveau style decorations are still a wonder to be seen. Today it still houses a wonderful mixture of restaurants and iconic shops, such as Langleys toy shop and the Colman's Mustard Shop and Museum.

St John's RC view south-east to Chapel Field Road in 1978.
Site of city wall marked on roundabout.

ENTERTAINMENT, LEISURE & PASTIMES

People can promenade by a river just as happily as they can along the sea front, as evidenced by this image of Riverside Road, next to the Wensum. The river on which our city stands is also a focal point for those who like to relax in a launch, rowing boat or skiff. Along with its companion, the Yare, our rivers and neighbouring broads offer plenty of opportunity to indulge in 'aquatic activities'. One very popular event takes place each year when rowers compete for the Carrow Cup in a contest that dates back to 1813 when boatmen would race for prize money.

Above: People came to Gorleston-on-Sea every summer so that they could enjoy a quiet British holiday in this small spot just below Great Yarmouth. Kiddies enjoyed the fun of sailing their toy boats in the children's yachting lake. Others went fishing off the small jetty, using a line wound round a square frame with mum's words ringing in their ears, 'Mind you take care not to fall in!' Marine Parade was popular with our parents as it was somewhere to stroll or just sit and enjoy looking at the gardens and golden sands. Such rest and relaxation was a grand release from the toil and turbulence of life back home. It is still a delightful place, so much quieter than its brasher neighbour.

Below: The Norwich Castle gardens provide a delightful oasis, tucked away next to a major piece of our city history. They are part of the old castle ditch and are often used as the site where theatrical productions are staged during the summer months. The castle itself was built as a royal palace by the Normans, being completed in the early 12th century. About 100 Saxon homes were demolished to create space for the building work; something that did not endear the invaders from over the Channel to local inhabitants. The keep was used as a gaol in the Middle Ages, providing a secure place for all manner of miscreants, ranging from debtors and petty felons right through to highwaymen and murderers.

Above: This is a picturesque view of the historic Earlham Plantation Garden, a creation of a prosperous Victorian businessman, Henry Trevor, who established a flourishing furniture and upholstery business in Norwich. He transformed the quarry just outside the old city walls into the three acre hidden garden we can see in this photograph. Seen in this photograph, the impressive Gothic revival fountain was his first creation. After the World War II the garden was virtually abandoned and overgrown and only used by children as a hideaway playground they nicknamed 'The Secret Garden'. Now restored, the Grade II listed gardens are again a source of pleasure for the people of Norwich.

Above right: These two images are views of the ABC cinema on Prince of Wales Road, in 1961, after it had been refurbished and renamed, when it changed from the Regent Theatre. Associated British Cinema had owned the business since 1929. The original Regent Theatre, a cine-variety establishment, was designed by architects G. Duncan Fitt with J. Owen Bond. The first film was 'the Prisoner of Zenda' on its opening night on 3 December, 1923. It also boasted a cafe and ballroom. Following successful business models in other cities the cinema tripled the number of screens in 1973. Several years later, a 74 video cinema was opened in the cafe area. Taken over by the Cannon Cinemas chain in April 1986, all four screens closed at the end of the 1990's and the interior was gutted and the balcony removed. The shell of the building was converted into a Nightclub which opened in 2003.

Above: Not a sole in sight as this photograph was taken in the city centre along Gentleman's Walk. The lone Ford Popular van is parked on the pavement next to the empty market stalls. It was July 1959 and sadly changes were afoot as the Gaumont Cinema was about to close and the building was to be demolished to make way for a new retail store. The original picture house opened on 18 February, 1911 as a conversion of a former London & Provincial Bank building. It became known as the Haymarket Picture House and in 1929 it became the sixth cinema in the UK to be equipped with 'sound on disc' equipment and it screened Al Jolson in "The Singing Fool". Around 1954 it was re-named the 'Gaumont' After the closure, the 'Gaumont' name was not lost as it was transferred to the Rank owned Carlton Cinema on All Saints Green.

Right: We can date this evening view of the Theatre De-Luxe accurately to 1934 as the film comedy showing was 'The Countess of Monte Cristo', starring Fay Wray, released in March of that year. The Theatre De-Luxe was the first picture palace in the city when it opened on 9 April, 1910. The cinema also became known as the 'ranch house', because of all the westerns it screened. It was very popular with the people of Norwich, so much so that in 1920 it was rebuilt to increase the number of seats to 1,000. It was the last cinema in Norwich to be converted to talking pictures in 1931 but the first to screen 3D films in 1953. For a few years after the end of the Second World War film-going boomed. Cinemas were modernised as new technology was applied to film making and projection. However, by the mid-1950s things were changing, the arrival of television was affecting cinemas in Norwich and across the country. The Theatre de Luxe was suffering and in 1957 it closed; its last night marred by vandalism.

THEATRE
DE-LUXE
THEATRE DE LUXE CINEMA
COUNTESS OF MONTE CRISTO
FAY WRAY
MONTE CRISTO
PATHETONE

These two pictures of the Hippodrome show by contrast, the up-beat, controversial era in the 1930s, to the downbeat pre-demolition stage of the building in the early 1960s. The Grand Opera House in St Giles' Street, as it was called originally, opened its doors for business for the first time on 3 August, 1903, with a musical play 'The Country Girl'. The theatre, designed by W G R Sprague, had been built on the site of the Norfolk Hotel and was set back from the street to allow carriages to deliver and collect the patrons.

Between both world wars, some of the greatest names in entertainment, such as Charles Chaplin, Marie Lloyd, and Gracie Fields, performed on the Hippodrome stage. In September of 1930 a deal was struck with A B C cinema's to take over the building to show films. One of the most controversial films screened was the German-made Morgenrot, in 1934, after the English ban on the film was lifted. The subject was naval warfare of the Great War and it was described as "a picture to abolish war."

In August 1937 the Hippodrome closed as a cinema and re-opened as a 'live' theatre. Despite receiving a direct hit during the 'Blitz' the theatre continued successfully and attracted household names such as Laurel and Hardy, Max Miller, Billy Cotton and Morecambe and Wise. By the mid-1950s, theatre audiences were in decline and it became a struggle to remain open. Despite a failed attempt to re-open as the Norfolk Playhouse, the Hippodrome continued until April 1960 when it closed for good. It was eventually demolished in 1964, making way for St. Giles Multi-storey Car Park, which opened two years later.

Above: Refitted in 1949, by the Norfolk Wherry Trust in order that at least one of these typically Norfolk trading vessels should continue to be seen plying its course along the County's rivers and broads. A 117yr old traditional Norfolk Wherry known as a 'black sailed trader', she is one of only two remaining trading barges built specifically for the Broads. At their peak there were over 300 of these craft. In the summer months during the Edwardian era, skippers scrubbed out the holds and took holiday makers for trips to make extra money. The Wherry Albion is seen here at Cow Tower proceeding along the Wensum on 14 October, 1949 - the day following its maiden voyage from Yarmouth to Norwich after having been refitted.

Right: This is a rare photograph from 1934, of the Capitol Cinema on Aylsham Road, approximately two years after it opened. Located in the Upper Hellesdon district, to the northwest of the city, opposite Glenmore Gardens, the 'Capitol' was opened on Boxing Day 1932 with Johnny Weismuller in the film "Tarzan the Ape Man". Adjacent to the cinema, just out of shot in this night time view was the Lido Swimming Pool, which also opened in the same year. Showing at the time were the 'George White's Scandals', a movie of Broadway revues produced by George White, which marked the film debut of Alice Faye. The Capitol Cinema was closed in April 1960. It was converted into the Lido Ballroom, later known as the Norwood Rooms. The front of the building was altered in the 1980's and it was converted into a Mecca Bingo Club, which extended itself into the adjacent former swimming pool.

These two photographs on Prince of Wales Road were taken almost 40 years apart. In the earliest image from 1919, we can see people going about their everyday life on the street outside the Norwich Electric Theatre. There is an electric tram in the distance but little evidence of other motorised transport on this stretch of road, with Rose Lane on the left and St Faiths Lane the first turn on the right. There is however some evidence on the road, that horses were used for business purposes. Down the centre of the thoroughfare we can also see the tramlines and the ornate gas lamps. The silent film 'The Man Who Forgot' is showing at the cinema, which was opened in 1912 as part of a chain of Electric Theatre's in the East Anglia region.

As life began to get back to normal after the Second World War, the cinema was given a total refurbishment and a name change to the Norvic Cinema. By the time of the second photograph in 1959, however, cinema audiences were in a steep decline, and despite the introduction of CinemaScope a few years earlier the cinema closed without notice. The film 'The Last Blitzkreig' could well have been one of the last films to be shown at the cinema before it closed its doors for the last time. It was subsequently demolished in 1961, and a modern red bricked office building stands on the site today.

This relaxed scene is from the home of the Anglo-American Club in St Clement vicarage. The photograph from February 1952 shows officers and WVS personnel mixing together in front of a roaring fire. Most are reading but they had the option also to play board games such as chess or listen to music from a state of the art Jukebox. During the Second World War, the 'Special Relationship' between the United Kingdom and the United States developed further long after the war had finished. It is unclear exactly why they have come together, it could be linked to intelligence work at RAF Watton or work carried out from RAF Lakenfield or perhaps just a training exercise in conjuction with the Women's Voluntary Service, who continued to operate as food rationing remained in place, funded from central government funds.

Fun for all the family in these photographs taken from around the opening of Waterloo Park in May 1933. Despite the overcast day, some of the younger ones are risking a dip in the icy waters of the paddling pool, while others are enjoying the swings and sand pit alongside. Waterloo Park can be found between Aylsham Road and Angel Road. It's one of a series of formal parks that received government funding after world war one. Today, it is Grade II* listed and is included in the English Heritage Register of Parks and Gardens of Special Historic Interest. In the second image we can see a wider area of the park, from an elevated position on top of the pavilion roof.

WORK & INDUSTRY

Adjacent to the present pedestrian bridge along Earlham Road stood the Grapes Hotel, a late Georgian house that had undergone various alterations at different times. 'the Grapes', was originally called the 'St Giles Gate' and first gained a licence in 1811. The tall building to the left of the Grapes was occupied by the Midland Bank and in the other half was Yaxley's wireless shop. To the right, on St Giles' Street was Hipperson's Dispensing Chemists. The photograph taken by George Plunkett was taken on 8 October, 1933, from the 'Tuns Inn' (now known as the Temple Bar),

when workmen were renewing the tram track. At St Giles' Gates the Unthank Road and Earlham Road routes converged with the route via Chapel Field North and Theatre Street. A mainly male crowd had gathered to watch proceedings, probably unemployed due to the depression when unemployment in Britain reached 22.8%, unaware that the whole system was to be abandoned little more than two years later.

This is the cattle market, though many of the animals we can see below look rather woolly! For centuries, this busy spot hummed with both the sound and smell of creatures brought in for sale in the shadow of Norwich Castle. Like many popular markets, there were a number of hostelries nearby where dealers and farmers could relax after a hard day's bargaining. The auctions were conducted in a lively and often humorous fashion. Above, is a much quieter scene from 1931, photographed from the Castle Hill, Bell Avenue area. This market closed in the 1960s and these streets disappeared under the Castle Mall shopping centre development.

Below: Seen from Southwell Road, this is the Queen's Road coal depot, as pictured in early April 1986. It had been part of the former Victoria Station, once the terminus of the Great Eastern main line. It was demolished in the 1970s. A branch of Sainsbury's now sits on this site and the trackbed has been converted into a pedestrian path and cycle route known as Lakenham Way. It is hard for a shopper to visualise now that she might be looking for carrots in an aisle where coal was once stored!

Claude Benton was the proprietor of this shop at 13 White Lion Street towards the end of February 1935. His chemist's was crammed full of all sorts of medicines and potions that professed to cure virtually any ailment known to man. His counters were piled up with elixirs, cough syrup, tablets and linctus. On the other side of his shop were display cabinets creaking under the weight of ointments, plasters and sprays. He also provided a friendly ear to listen to all the aches and pains that Aunt Cissie described to him.

Broads Tours

Relaxing days on the water

There can be few holiday experiences that consistently live up to their billing. But a trip with Broads Tours is one that delivers everything it promises. One reason for that is the experience behind the name.

Broads Tours was established in 1935 by Charles Hannaford who operated passenger boats under the name Norfolk Broads Tours Company. Within a year, Hannaford had formed a new company, Broads Tours and Services (Wroxham) Ltd and commissioned the building of an impressive craft for the princely sum of £1,000.

The boat, made of mahogany with a length of 56ft, was named the Marina, sister ship to the Marchioness.

***Above:** Some of the Broads Tours fleet in 1962.*

That was the beginning of one of the most popular attractions in the country and by the 1950s Broads Tours was enjoying a boom period with more and more people flocking to the Broads for a day out.

The Broads Tours fleet continued to expand and two wooden boats were added to the fleet, the Princess Anne and Princess Alexandra.

The business changed its name to Broads Tours and launched more boats including the first double-decker passenger cruiser, The Cordon Rouge. Commissioned by the then new owner of the business, Len Funnel, it quickly became a local landmark.

In 2003 the company was bought by the Greasley family - Paul, Barbara and their two children, Laura and James. The family still run Broads Tours today along with a team of experienced skippers and crew members.

"We have been proud to carry on the fantastic work that Charles Hannaford began all those years ago," said Barbara. "During this time we have built a new double-decker passenger boat and four luxury day cruisers and have shared this special area with hundreds of thousands of visitors."

The company operates a full timetable using four double-decker passenger boats between April and the end of October and hosts evening music cruises and chartered celebration trips for anyone marking a special occasion.

"We take enormous pride in being able to supply people of all ages and abilities a truly magical experience on the Norfolk Broads," said Barbara.

***Left:** One of Broads Tours impressive passenger cruisers, the 'Queen of the Broads', pictured in 2012.*

BBC Fire Protection

Firm's products are life-savers

They go about their business quietly and efficiently. You only know they are there in times of extreme emergency but the products and services marketed by BBC Fire Protection Ltd are, quite literally, life-savers.

BBC was founded in 1979 by Norfolk man Nicholas Copeman supported by his father-in-law Fred Bushell. It was run from a former corner shop in Cyprus Street, Norwich, by Mr Copeman, his wife Erica, and sister-in-law Angela Kelly.

Mr Copeman, in charge of operations and business development, had worked for a local fire extinguisher company for four years before striking out on his own supported by Mr Bushell as chairman, Mrs Kelly, business administrator, and Mrs Copeman, customer services. Founding directors were Mr Copeman, Mr Bushell and the late Mr Roger Burr who played an invaluable part in the early days of the company, focusing on the technical and contracting elements.

"We combine expert knowledge of our field with a commitment to attentive, personal service," says Mr Copeman.

"Our customers know that by choosing BBC they are investing in an individual solution, not just a piece of equipment."

By 1984, the company's continued expansion necessitated a move to bigger premises – a factory unit and offices in Diamond Road.

The move prompted the installation of its first computer network instigated by Martin Church, now company secretary and director, which revolutionised the management of the business.

In the beginning fire alarm systems largely comprised of simple, non-intelligent devices obtained from relatively low-tech sources.

Today, the products are intelligent microprocessor sensors that can be controlled from computers, smartphones and the web.

Mr Copeman used his experience to develop the business and look at new ways of supplying, installing and maintaining active fire safety systems and equipment. The goal was to offer customers complete assurance of quality and build on their reputation that they could be trusted for any assignment.

High profile contracts, such as equipping Windsor Castle with fire detection and alarm systems between 1987 and 1997, a period which spanned the catastrophic blaze in November, 1992, increased the firm's standing.

That message was pressed home by John Standen who joined the business soon after the company's incorporation as a director with responsibility for the service operation.

The company quickly grew locally and nationally to become one of the leaders in its field. The recipe for success looks deceptively simple.

By appointment to
H.M. Queen Elizabeth
Purveyors of
Fire Protection Systems

Right: *By Royal appointment.*

Above and left: *From a former corner shop to purpose-built headquarters, St Florian House, Wymondham.*

'We do not want to just sell our customers a system. We want to provide them with a solution and a service. Others have to sell you the system they have, not because it's best for them but because it's the only one they have!'

Nick Copeman, Operations Director

Due to the company's continued work at Sandringham House, BBC was appointed by HM Queen Elizabeth ll as 'purveyors of fire protection systems' in 1986. Today, BBC is still a proud holder of the Royal Warrant which next year will be for 30 concsecutive years.

By virtue of the company's pedigree in working in royal households, BBC was selected to install a new fire detection and voice alarm system to the home of the Prime Minister, 10 Downing Street.

The business was growing quickly and by 2004, with ambitious plans for the future, the need for bigger premises was critical and a move to purpose-built premises at St Florian House, Wymondham, was undertaken.

Retail stores have always been important customers and in 2005 BBC received its first £1 million contract to design and install a fire detection and alarm system into Selfridges flagship department store in Oxford Street, London.

As well as Selfridges, other famous names who turn to BBC for their fire protection systems include Debenhams, House of Fraser, Argos, Homebase and Iceland.

Above: *Investing in staff and equipment has kept BBC at the forefront of fire prevention and detection.*

Project profile: Aviva

BBC Fire was engaged to design, supply and install the fire detection and alarm package for this large, critical data handling and storage facility.

Working to a tight and demanding programme, BBC Fire met and delivered to the clients requirements and expectations. After the successful contract BBC was awarded the planned maintenance of the system through the client's Facility Managers.

While retail tops the list, other headings forming BBC's main markets both in the UK and abroad, include heritage, waste recycling, data centres, social housing, construction and defence.

One of the firm's most outstanding achievements was meeting United States Air Force specifications for fire alarms in dormitories.

Above: *Safety first at Canary Wharf.*
Right: *BBC fitted fire alarm systems at Norwich City Football Club.*

"We developed a unique solution which brought contracts to the business worth millions of pounds" said Mr Copeman.

The list of high profile projects undertaken by BBC is endless and covers a wide range of assignments. It includes protecting Norwich Cathedral from ground level to the tip of its spire, installing fire alarm systems for football club rivals Norwich City and Ipswich Town and fitting a voice alarm system in the 45-floor (656ft) HSBC Tower in Canary Wharf.

The company also developed a central fire reporting system which enables large defence sites to receive fire alarm indications at a

Above and right: *Celebrating 20 years.*

'The specification of fire protection systems is a crucial business with the ultimate aim of saving lives and protecting property. So much peace of mind is gained from having the trust and security of a stable, tightly-knit business.'

Nick Copeman, Operations Director

central security building which has led to valuable contracts worth hundreds of thousands over a 10-year period.

Recent projects include installing systems in a number of large independent and private schools throughout the UK and winning a contract for new fire alarms for the new Japanese owners of the British Broadcasting Corporation 'Bush House' building, for years the home of the World Service.

BBC employs a team of skilled craftsmen which ensures continuity on any task. The company not only installed new fire alarms in the Tower of London but also lifted and refitted all the floorboards, most of them several hundreds of years old – all part of the service.

The key to BBC's continued success is its people. While the workforce has risen from four to 104 the family business ethos remains strong.

"While many of our peers have been subject to takeovers we have remained defiantly independent," said Mr Copeman. "Many of our senior management team have been with us since inception keeping abreast of new technologies while at the same time remaining a recognisable point of contact for clients.

"This has enabled the development of close relationships over the years. Staff share a common belief in the importance of their work and while their professional credentials are second-to-none their personal qualities also reflect company standards.

"In every area of the company the focus is on satisfied customers," said Mr Copeman.

Above and below: *Highly skilled staff with some of the equipment that BBC supply and install.*

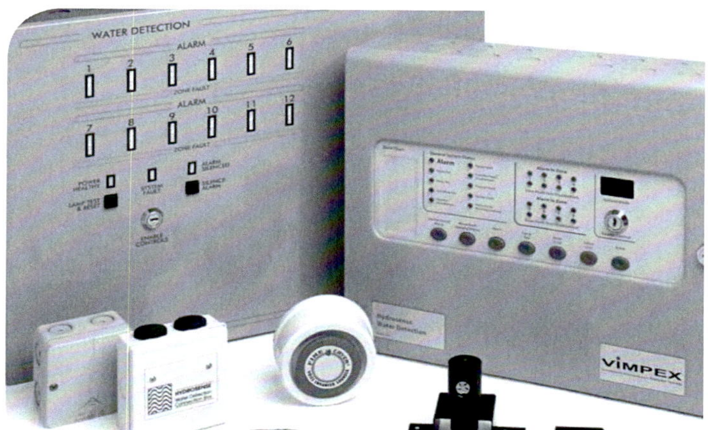

Bowhill & Elliott
Traditional skills, a unique product

Handmade shoes have been sold from 65, London Street, Norwich, since 1843. They remain highly sought after by loyal customers for whom quality is a byword.

One of the forerunners of the present firm was Wright and Co run by Robert Wright in partnership with Mr W. Base.

At the same time Obadiah Henry Bowhill, who was making shoes in Pottergate near to the cathedral, was beginning to take an interest in the more established business and bought it in 1874.

Two of his four sons entered into business with him while his daughter married Thomas Baines Elliott. Obadiah sold the business to his son, also Obadiah, and together they formed Bowhill & Elliott in 1897.

The family connection continues today with the business under the direction of Roger Jury. Roger's Great Great Grandmother was Margaret Elliott, born in 1833. Margaret Elliott was Thomas Baines Elliott's Aunt.

Above: *Bowhill & Elliott's eye-catching shop front in about 1930.*

Bowhill & Elliott built on Obadiah's firm foundations of making footwear for professional, business and farming families all with their own special requirements for indoor and outdoor use. Such a variety of clientele enabled the partners to provide for older customers as well as adding a touch of style for younger ones.

The turn of the century saw the firm making large quantities of bespoke riding boots for army officers and during the South African War Bowhill & Elliott supplied the ankle boots and leather gaiters that were essential wear for the troops.

Many young men who had shoes made before leaving home to make their way in the colonies ordered their military boots from Bowhill & Elliott on the outbreak of war in 1914. This was a simple matter as all good bootmakers retained their customers' lasts - a mechanical form that has a shape similar to that of a human foot used by shoemakers in the manufacture and repair of shoes.

Following the return to peace time trading the firm continued to make shoes to order, supplying pupils at Norwich Grammar and Suffield Park Schools. Having overcome the Depression the family was able to deal with the military demands of the Second World War – indeed, it was these that kept business going in the difficult days of rationing materials with any military value.

One of Bowhill & Elliott's trademark products are the supremely comfortable hand-turned slippers originally made by the Osoeasie Slipper Company founded by Jack Hale in 1939. This originated in the former Enterprise Picture House and was carried on after his death by his widow until 1960 when Bowhill & Elliott bought the business.

Today, the company splits its operation equally between retail and manufacturing employing 17 people, both full-time and part-time. On the retail side of the business they sell men's and women's shoes and the Bowhill & Elliott slippers.

Left: *An early advertisement for Bowhill & Elliott taken from a 1926 edition of Roberts & Co's Norwich Almanac*

Men's shoes include leading brands such as Crockett & Jones, Joseph Cheaney, Barkers and Loake, all high quality welted shoes made in and around Northampton. Prices start at £220. Women's makes include continental brands such as Peter Kaiser, Brunate, Gabor, Mephisto and HB Shoes.

Retail customers are mostly local to Norfolk who understand and appreciate good quality footwear. A small quantity of slippers are sold from London Street and online via their website. The vast majority of the products are sold to other high quality retailers in London, across Europe, New York, Japan and Hong Kong. The biggest market is London and about 40 per cent of production goes for export.

Maintaining hand craft skills is the priority, according to Roger Jury.

"There are many challenges facing small, independent businesses, particularly in manufacturing, We have to maintain the craft skills which are unique to our business."

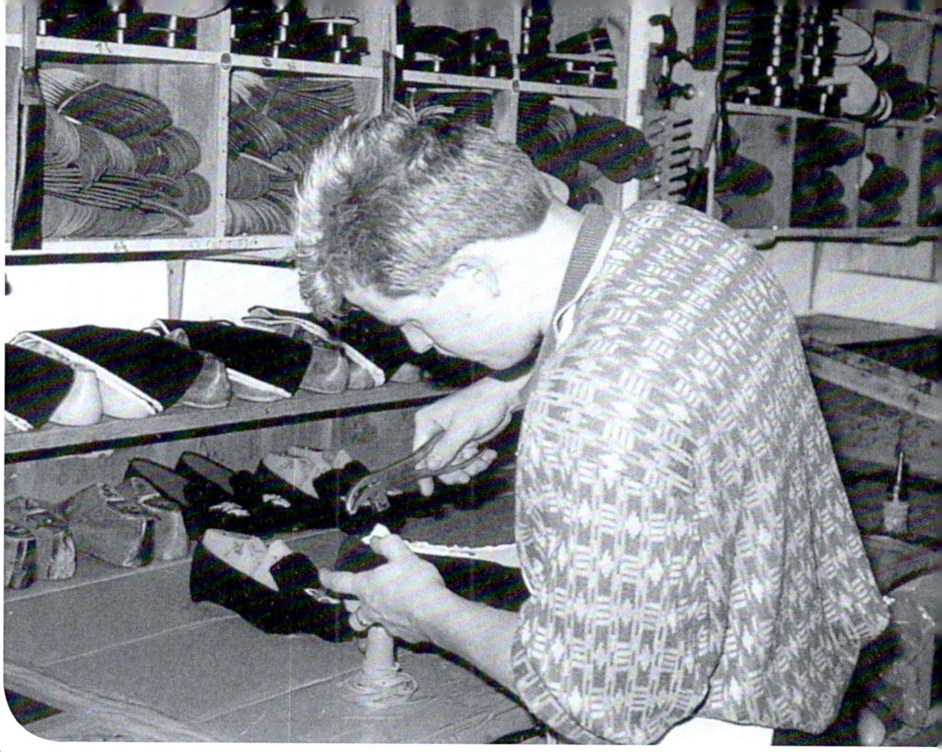

Above and below: *Bowhill & Elliott craftsmen at work on the highly-skilled art of hand lasting.* ***Inset:*** *Roger Jury demonstrating hand lasting at a recent heritage open day.*

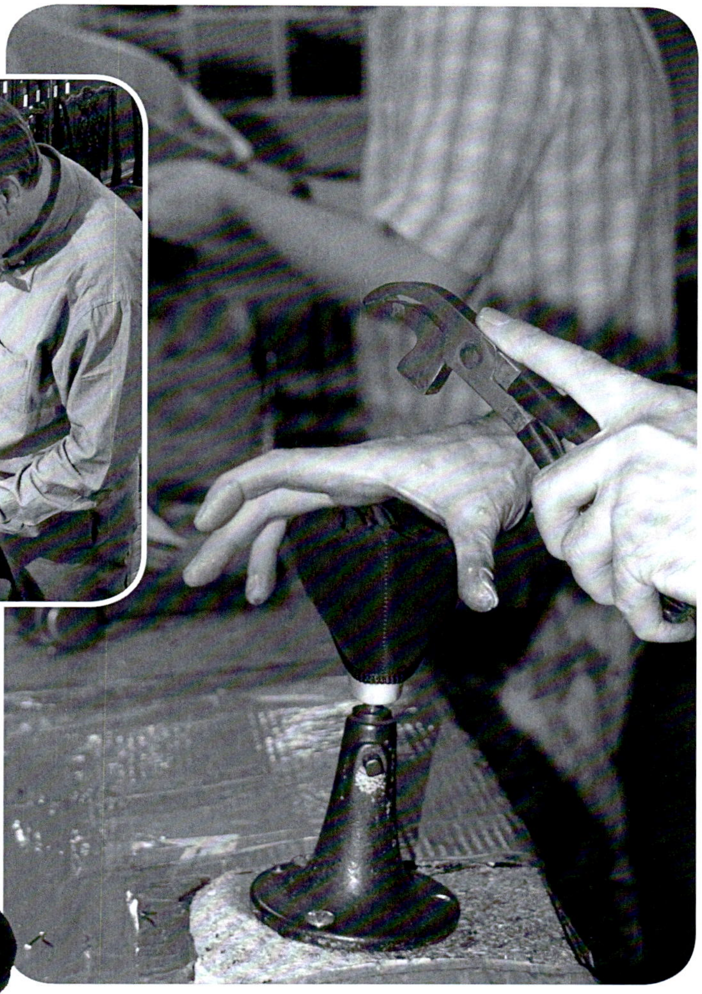

He said the company prides itself on retaining a traditional style of working, using modern technology only as a means to an end to allow more time hand-making the products they sell.

The most popular product is the hand embroidered and hand made slipper, made mostly from velvet with a quilted satin lining.

"We often get feedback from customers saying that these are the most comfortable shoes they have ever worn," said Roger. "They also like the fact that they can individualise their slippers with unique embroidered designs. No two pairs need ever be alike."

Below: *Velvet slippers with rampant lion (left) and personalised monogram.*

ACKNOWLEDGMENTS

The publishers would like to give a special thanks to Jonathan Plunkett and his family for providing the majority of the photographs in this publication from his fathers astonishing collection.

George Plunkett compiled an unbelievable pictorial archive of photographs which stretches right back to the 1930s. He was born in Norwich, and from 1931 to 2006, built a comprehensive photographic survey of the city and further afield. The archive includes around 3600 black-and-white photographs and we are delighted to have been able to use just a small selection in this Norwich publication.

Flood level gauges New Mills Yard from August 1961. Recording Norwich Flood levels 1570-1912. The young boy in the picture is Jonathan and he is the younger son of the photographer George Plunkett.

All reasonable steps were taken by the publishers of this book to trace the copyright holders and obtain permissions to use the photographs contained herein. However, due to the passage of time certain individuals were untraceable. Should any interested party subsequently come to light, the publishers can be contacted at the phone number printed at the front of this book and the appropriate arrangements will then be made.